What others a

In a world which seems to harbor so much indifference, injustice, cruelty and violence, these words of patience, forgiveness and love beckon the reader to an oasis of hope in the parched sands of hopelessness.

> —Captain Jerry Coffee, author of *Beyond Survival*

The strong spirit of love that permeates this book will indeed bring hope and healing to many people.

> —D. Trinidad Hunt, author of *The Operator's Manual for Planet Earth—An Adventure for the Soul*

I was deeply touched by this book.

> —Rebecca Maddox, author of *Inc. Your Dreams*

Warm, evocative and healing words to soothe and nurture the spirit.

> —Charles Martin, Ph.D., C.A.P.T., Gainesville, Florida

As a pastoral counselor for 40 years, I find this book amazing in its openness to the transforming love of God.

> — Rev. Douglas Olson, Calvary by the Sea Lutheran Church

Relax in its comfort. Be energized by its truths. *From Pain To Joy* is a balm that will help make the wounded whole.

> —Ian Percy, author of *Going Deep: Exploring Spirituality in Life and Leadership*

From Pain to Joy

Dear Marilyn,
Love + Aloha,
Nan Hanson
595. 1958
nanhan@aol.com

Also by the author
Create Work You Love

From Pain to Joy

INSPIRING WORDS
FOR HOPE AND HEALING

Nancy Hanson

The anecdotes in this book are composites inspired by the profiles of many people. None of these is meant to represent any one individual.

From Pain to Joy. Copyright © 1998 by Nancy Hanson.
All rights reserved. Printed in the U.S.A. on recycled paper.
Pages of this book may be photocopied.
Published by Career Discovery, Honolulu, Hawaii.

Design by Dale Vermeer

Hanson, Nancy.
    From pain to joy : inspiring words for hope and healing
    / Nancy Hanson.--1st ed.
    p. cm.
    Includes bibliographical references.
    Preassigned LCCN: 98-3854
    ISBN: 0-9644736-9-0

    1. Meditations. 2. Prayers. 3. Joy --Religious
aspects. 4. Spiritual healing. I. Title.

BL560.H36 1999   291.4′3
                                  QBI98-1280

THIS BOOK IS DEDICATED

TO THE STILL,

SMALL VOICE THAT HELPS

US DEAL WITH

LIFE'S PAIN, THAT GIVES US

LOVE, PEACE, JOY AND

GUIDANCE.

CONTENTS

Foreword
Acknowledgements
Introduction

CONTENTS

Foreword

I first met Nancy Hanson at the University of Hawaii where she was teaching a self-publishing class. It didn't take long to realize that her gift of knowledge was matched by a generosity of spirit in helping other people achieve their goals.

To know Nancy and to work with her in releasing emotional blocks has truly been a life-changing experience for me. I acknowledge Nancy for her love of life, dedication to God and willingness to share her heartfelt truth in this book.

Mahalo,
Michael D. Morrison, I.C.A.K., F.I.A.C.A., C.N.H.P., D.C.

Living on Maui, Dr. Morrison writes about and teaches intuitive kinesiology to facilitate health-conscious people in healing the mind, body and spirit.

Acknowledgements

My most profound thanks go to God. To feel the words of a higher power come through me is an honor and grace gift.

I am also extremely grateful for the encouragement received from Joy Appleton and Judy Gorman. Early on, they each read a few chapters and told me to share this with others as soon as possible. Jana Wolff supports me as only a true friend can; she honors my beliefs even when she doesn't share some of them.

At the Maui Writers Conference I met my agent, Nancy Ellis, whose faith in this project motivated me to keep writing.

God used the life experience and kindness of many good souls to review chapters and add their edits, comments and/or hurrahs. Thank you to: Ann Arnone, Michele Belanger, Dr. Arne Benz, Wanda Buckmaster, Pam Chambers, Annabel Chotzen, Sashi Dhar, Valla Dana Fotiades, Kim Gordon, Ann Griffen, Judy Hamacher, Linda Hansen, Cathy Heflin, Sam Horn, Rev. David Hustoft, Debbie Jenae, Rick Kendig, Betty Ling, Elizabeth Lindsey, Susan Leuning, Nancy Lundsgaard, Lorraine Mackay, Rebecca Maddox, Paula Mantel, Shannon McMonagle, Jeff Morosetti, Kate Muller, Julie Nelson, Rev. Doug Olson, Barbara Trandem, Deb Pimental, Manning Richards, Nancy Riesz, Linda Rinaldi, Tom and Jodi Rogness-Sheldon, Lolly Shim, Susanne Sims, Dottie Sunio, Lorraine Teniya and Torrance Trevorrow.

Thanks to Dale and Mari Vermeer for creating such an appealing cover design and layout.

The love and support I receive from my husband, Jerol Hanson, are priceless.

Introduction

When you are in a personal relationship with God, you will have less pain and more joy. I know this to be true from my own experience and have highlighted in this book some of the infinite number of ways in which God provides guidance to those who seek hope and healing.

God longs to be in communion with you. One way to be in this partnership is described in the first section. The remaining chapters are about how the pain in specific situations can be transformed into joy. In Section Two, you will learn how to have more satisfaction and less anguish in your earthly relationships.

Having been a career counselor for the last ten years, I am aware of the distress that comes with career and life transition. Issues such as being laid off, looking for a job and getting older are addressed in Section Three.

The suffering described in Section Four is of those who have been hurt by certain judgments given in God's name and, in my opinion, without God's permission. For example, people who choose to have an abortion or who practice an alternative sexual lifestyle are sometimes told that they are sinners and will go to hell unless they repent for their sins. Those who divorce are sometimes chastised.

Section Five is dedicated to those who are affected by the agony that comes with addiction. You will read about the special problems relationships have when one or both of the partners are in recovery.

Lastly, Section Six is for people who want more peace and less strife in life areas which challenge us in terms of patience, balance, learning disorders, or life-threatening illness.

Questions and emotions may surface as you read this book. If you would like help in the process of working through such feelings, you may want to meet with a professional counselor, pastor or rabbi. You may also choose to join a support group, church, synagogue or meditation center.

With my first thoughts of writing the book, I received a clear message to use a first person format. Hopefully you will get used to this intimate style. When the spirit speaks to me, I often hear "we" as in "We are thrilled" and "We love you." Perhaps the pronoun "we" is used to signify that God is a plural energy available to all of us at all times.

Picture God as being in your heart and mind, rather than being "out there." If you have previously felt alienated or condemned, you can come to feel accepted and welcomed by this spirit within you.

Those of you familiar with scripture will see evidence of my Christian upbringing when you read biblical references in several of the chapters. Having a spiritual union is what has given me guidance, love, peace and joy for most of my life. I pray that this book can be a vehicle for you to receive the same and more.

With love and aloha,
Nancy Hanson

THE PURPOSE OF THIS BOOK

IS TO HELP YOU

SEE GOD IN A NEW WAY.

section one

The Journey

How to go from pain to joy

"WE" is God.

Welcome to *From Pain to Joy*. We are thrilled for an opportunity to speak with you. We want you to receive our love, peace, joy and guidance. Some of you are ready to jump in and read. Others of you are wondering: "Who is this voice and where is it coming from? Why should I believe that it is God?"

Good questions. The voice in this book represents the universal spirit that has been given many names throughout history. A common name for this spirit is God and that is the name used here. We hope that as you read, you will hear more than what is written. You may want to read with a pen and paper at hand. If you have a question about something, please write it down. May you hear our answers to your questions as you open your mind and meditate on our presence in your life. For now, sit back and let us speak with you about how to travel on the journey from pain to joy.

You may need healing

You will receive our joy when you are in a personal relationship with us. If you have been told that you are a sinner and that we will send you to hell unless you repent, your picture of us is probably not a positive one. In our name you may have been ridiculed, condemned or made to feel guilty. These are hurts that need to be treated.

You may need spiritual healing of your feeling of separation from us. We are not referring to physical healing because there are people with cancer and other ailments who, even in their distress, experience a divine connection.

If you have a negative image of us, we'd like this to change. We created you. We love you. We want the best for you. From now on, practice seeing us as a loving presence in your life. Nothing you could do will ever separate you from our love. We are generous, abundant, all-knowing, all-powerful and always present. Although you may never fully grasp the awesomeness of who we are, please start viewing us in a positive way.

The second kind of healing we offer you is healing of your emotional pain. When you have feelings such as sadness, hurt, anger and disappointment, tell us your story by thinking, writing or speaking with us. We understand what you are going through. Of course, we don't expect you to be happy all the time. We do, however, hope that you come to us and receive our comfort.

We also heal you of guilt. Through faith in our ability to forgive, you will experience the complete release of your guilt. It may come back and we are always present to remove it once again. Christians receive forgiveness through a belief that Christ died on the cross to make an atonement for all of their sins. Some Buddhists experience our healing through meditating on the compassionate face of the Bodhisattva. We give you many ways to experience our forgiveness and our healing.

Living in our healing power is an important ongoing spiritual activity. You may need healing today because of your wounded self-esteem or negative self-image. You may need healing of your angry, hurtful thoughts. Ask us to heal you. Picture our loving spirit dwelling within you, ready to soothe all pain. See your hurts as burdens that we literally lift from you. This is one way in which we heal. You will experience our perfect love which casts out fear. You will go from pain to joy as you ask for, acknowledge and receive by faith our presence in your life.

A story of hurt and healing

Let us tell you a mother's story: "My 24-year-old daughter had just finished her second year as a special education teacher when she was killed in a car accident. The priest told me that she would go to hell because she was not a virgin. God, can this really be?" We long to tell her that those words from the priest are not from us. Her daughter is not in or going to hell. We want to give this woman peace about her daughter.

We will heal as soon as the mother becomes receptive to our voice. If she does not give us an opening, she will suffer by believing such a message.

With your faith, we will heal the negative image you once had of us. Now, let's talk more about hearing our voice.

Listen to our voice within you

You may already know that you have a life force inside. You have, at least once, felt some sort of intuition leading you. We are that positive force. At times, you may sense that we are giving you a message. There are other times when you have difficulty hearing our voice. Perhaps you are afraid that we will tell you to sell everything you own and become a missionary. Could it be that a part of you does not feel worthy to hear our voice? You may be thinking, "Who do I think I am to say that I hear God's voice?" Some people think, "If there is a living God of all the universes, why would such a God talk with me?"

There are those of you who know you are worthy, who are not afraid, and you are still not hearing our voice. Please be patient. Believe that we are present and desire to have communion with you. Why? Because we created you. We want you to know you are never alone. We want to guide you and shower you with love.

Some of you sense our presence when you see beauty. The feeling of awe you have is your heart telling you that there is a creator. We are just as much with you in your living room as we are with you in the mountains and meadows.

We want connection with everyone. Picture our spirit hovering around you. That may sound unusual, but we are truly present. We make all the difference between feeling alone and feeling connected; feeling afraid and feeling peaceful; feeling self critical and feeling loved.

It may take time for you to hear our voice. Start this way: Imagine what we *would* say if you *could* hear us. The next time you have a choice to make, talk with us as if we were able to answer you... because we are. We have a wise, still, small voice that gently nudges you. Look and listen for us.

What if you hear more than one voice? Which voice is from us? We start by letting you know how much we love you. When you sense that you are getting more than one answer, this is a sign for you to slow down. Give us more time in introspection and contemplation and a clear knowing will come to you. Sometimes you are quick to seek answers from others rather than from us. Well-meaning people will lead you in a way that is not our best way for you. Try us first. Your faith will develop as you grow in sensing our direction.

There are times when we will guide you to break through a fear. We will tell you, for example, to say "no" to abuse or to say "yes" to a joy that you previously denied yourself. Then we show you how. Read chapter three for an example of how we lead you to say yes to joy. In chapter six you will see how we can help you make choices for a healthier family life. There may also be periods of silence. Go ahead and make plans anyway. Know we are leading you, even when you don't feel our guidance. Blessed are those who don't see or hear and yet still believe.

Although there is no one right way to start this listening process, there is one vital ingredient necessary for you to start hearing our voice. Time. We want time with you in daily meditation. During this quiet time, ask for our will and to be filled with our presence.

What does it feel like to be in communion with us? Think of a time when you have felt the most loved by a friend, spouse, parent, or another family member. You are being totally cared for. Sometimes you are aware of our presence at a worship service filled with people. Other times, you will be by yourself. We love being connected with you and want you to know our presence. When you experience our healing and when you are in communication with us, you are moving from pain to joy.

Some of you are still perplexed. You want to know exactly how to talk with us. Are you being led by us to quit your job, or are you just getting tired? Some people ask us for a good parking place. Sometimes they actually get one. Other times they don't. When they get it they say, "Praise The Lord." When they don't get it, they say, "It wasn't God's will." What is this all about?

One way to hear our voice is to ask specific questions, and when you are silently listening, the answers will come. These answers may not always be logical, but they will feel true and right, even if difficult. Take the answer you think you got from us and record it in a journal. Whether or not you follow our suggestion, keep track of what you think might have happened if you had followed it. After a while, your need to test us will be gone. For now, it is okay to be skeptical.

Remember, sometimes there will be silence, which does not mean we are absent. We may have already provided you with the ability to find the answer. We are within you.

Hearing our voice

Nan hears us when she quiets her soul in meditation, usually in the early morning. Then she will get on the computer and type out questions such as: "Lord, what do you want me to accomplish today?" "I feel bad about a comment I made yesterday; what shall I do?" For years she has gotten specific answers that range from instructions on how to best help a friend to what clothes to pack for a trip. There are times when she does not get clear direction. When this happens, Nan is usually detached and faithful regarding our timing. She experiences the security of knowing that she is never alone and that she is connected to the greatest source of wisdom and comfort there is.

You may choose to use the computer, a pad of paper or nothing at all. The main thing is to start listening. Daily communication with us is not something you must do. It is something you want to do because it is a source of joy and guidance.

Joy in the journey—even during the hard times

What are your thoughts about joy? Some people think, "Part of life includes the hard stuff, like: when I hurt someone's feelings or someone hurts mine; when I overdraw the checking account; when I get in a car accident; or when I find out that my father has cancer. To always enjoy life is not possible." We are not saying that you should yell, "Praise God" immediately when trouble comes. What we are saying is that we help you accept and then rise above the circumstances.

When you are acknowledging us in your thoughts and heart, nothing can happen that will separate you from our love. What happens when a tragedy comes? We weep with you when you weep. You have the option of either leaving or staying close to us in these difficult times. When you choose to stay close, there is more peace than with any other choice.

When bad things happen to you, please come to us right away. Literally feel our arms around you providing comfort. Sense our all-knowing, all-powerful presence taking care of you. When you know that we are within you, the hardest problem is not as bad as it would be if you were alone. You can even get to a point of saying to us, "Oh Lord, how are we going to handle this one?" Knowing that we are with you gives an optimism in even the worst of situations. When you partner with us, you will experience an inner joy, no matter what happens.

Let us repeat, that to live with joy does not mean that you will be happy all the time. When you know that we are in you, a peace that passes all understanding will fill you. In chapter 25 you will read about feeling our presence no matter what the circumstances.

Accept, love and embrace yourself...today

The next step for you in your journey from pain to joy is to take the notion of self-love very seriously. Here is where we joyously shout: There is only one you. Love, accept and embrace yourself. Then, discover, develop and share who you are with the world. Individuals who know and use their gifts have their share of hard times. For the most part, though, they enjoy themselves and their lives. We want this for you.

We ache when you hate yourself. We long for you to be able to look in the mirror, smile and even laugh. You can love and accept yourself when you realize that we were involved in your creation. As soon as you ask us, we will help you to start loving yourself. We'll show you the blocks that need to be removed so that you can grow in self-acceptance. Your self-love will increase as you discover your uniqueness. Recall the talents, gifts and skills you use when you are having the most fun. This could be when you repaired an engine, researched a health issue or solved a complex problem. Some get joy from teaching, coaching or counseling. Giving a loving look or touch can bring as much or more satisfaction than receiving one. Creators are thrilled when they've written a song, crafted a chest of drawers or designed a building. Perhaps you're a great host who can plan and organize an event from start to finish.

You will need to get training to do some of the things you've identified. Other activities you have listed are ones that you can do today. The point is that we created you to discover, develop and enjoy yourself. It may be tempting, but surely not rewarding, to try to be someone else.

We would like you to get your validation from us, not from the world. There will always be someone who doesn't approve of you and what you are doing. Look to us and we will give you support for you to be you. The next time you feel you are not good enough, not attractive enough, not smart enough or not whatever enough, please stop. Invite us to help you love, accept and embrace the you that we created.

Four aspects of the journey

We have just shown you four parts of the journey from pain to joy: You may need healing. Listen to our voice within you. Handle the hard stuff with us. Love and accept yourself.

In the following chapters, we show how you can go from pain

to joy in specific life situations. We'll discuss each issue and help you apply it to your own life. We'll give you action steps. Each chapter ends with a prayer so that you can commune with us. Talking and listening are essential parts of a relationship. You may read this book straight through or go to the chapter you can't wait to read. Each chapter has the same message: When you are in a relationship with us, we lead you from pain to joy.

An open invitation

"WE" is God.

You may be interested in spirituality. You may believe in us to some degree. You may already utter a "Thank you, God" when good things happen. But, you aren't sure about engaging in this dialogue that is being encouraged.

You might be wondering something like, "If I don't choose to have a relationship with God, am I going to hell?" Our purpose in this book is to help you learn how to accept, know, love and live with us. We are not in the condemning business, contrary to popular belief. We are kindness, gentleness, patience and faithfulness. We love you with an unconditional love. There is nothing you can do that will separate yourself from us.

Take all the time you need to read, wrestle and research how you want to view us, and how you want to relate with us.

A few actions you could take in your exploration:
- Talk with us, even if it feels as if you are talking to the air.
- Know that it is impossible to fail in this experiment. You will only learn.
- Practice living in our loving presence.
- Ask us to help remove any block you may have in relating with us.
- You may want to pray the following:

Dear God,
   I'm not even sure if you hear me when I pray! Sometimes I feel as if I don't have a clue about who you are. I've had concepts of who

you might be, and it is all rather intriguing and confusing to me.

I have a hunch that there could be spiritual healing for me and for my pain. I also have a hunch that you have something to do with joy. I am open to learning. It's just that I feel somewhat trapped by the phrase, "Be in a relationship with God."

I don't like the idea of someone thrusting his or her form of spirituality on me. I've had this happen in the past. Many people are so sure of what is right, that now I am wary.

For example, it sounds like I am getting a message that if I don't engage in a personal relationship with you, then I am not doing the spiritually right thing. This doesn't sit well with me. Is there truly only one way? I don't think so.

Well, Lord, I am willing to see what you have to say. But, how do I know that these words are really from you? Now, that may be my biggest question. Have I gone off the deep end by even reading a book like this? God speaking to me through a book? Well, stranger things have happened. I know they have.

Lord, I like the phrase, "I believe, help my unbelief." I'm thankful that you are a God of acceptance, forgiveness, peace, everlasting love, joy, kindness, gentleness, patience and faithfulness. With skepticism and faith, I will take my time deciding how I want to engage in our relationship. There's a part of me that is already relating with you. Part of me wants to go deeper. I'm also wondering if I want to give you the time. These are my considerations. I trust that you will help me handle them. Thank you. Amen.

section two

Relationships

Is there some joy out there that I'm missing?

"WE" is God who is within you.

There is more delight to be experienced than you are even aware of. Why are some happier than others? Being in a personal, daily, intimate relationship with us is the key. We lead you to joy and friendship in a variety of ways. Let's look at Jan's story.

As a married woman, Jan figured that attraction to anyone other than her husband was probably not a good idea. Then she met Dave. Within two hours a magical connection happened. We consistently led her to develop a friendship with him. Through getting to know Dave, she felt a new joy and aliveness. This enhanced love of life spilled into all her relationships and gave her more caring, trust and warmth for her husband than ever before. Dave moved to Canada and they have little contact anymore. Still, this friendship will last a long time.

Jan loved Dave's honesty, humility, faith, humor, quick mind, vulnerability and kindness. She was inspired by his attitude about life. He was handsome, too. Part of her lesson to learn was that it can be positive to feel affinity. She did not have to buy in to the idea that she should feel guilty for her attraction. Rather, she learned that the more love you freely give, the more we give you to share.

Jan increased her time of prayer and listening to us earlier that year and learned to have greater trust in our leading. Many times, Jan experienced our voice telling her specifics as in, "Call him." Jan doubted our guidance and wanted to get outside advice. Some of her friends thought it was a wonderful new relationship and a few others cautioned her to not pursue it. We told her to go for the joy in this new friendship. When you dedicate your life to us, we gladly return to you fun, learning, newness, awe, joy, creativity, meaning and the feeling of being alive. This is what happened for Jan.

Come to your heart and listen. We will never lead you to embarrassment, evil or danger. We lead you to what is best for you.

Following our leading, even when it felt uncomfortable, Jan went from anxiety to glee. At the heart of Jan's worry was her low self-esteem. "If he's such a great guy, why would he want to spend time with me? What if I call him and he has no interest in talking with me? What if we get together and I say or do something stupid? What if we have a good time together, then what?" These kinds of concerns could be keeping you from going for the joy. Listen to our voice. We'll help you cross your barriers. We helped Jan develop the friendship even when she felt nervous. Jan also noticed that as soon as she followed our leading, the worry would leave.

Are you wondering how to deal with one of your fears? This could be doing a job or field interview, calling for a first date, asking for a raise or writing a letter to an estranged parent or child. In your heart, ask us if we'd like you to make the next move, then listen. There will be a peaceful knowing.

Is there something happening in your life where you have the attitude, this feels so good that it must be wrong? Take the time to let your heart speak rather than the rules you've been raised with. Sometimes it really does feel right. Other times, it does not. Learn to be led by our spirit. There are times when Jan still has trouble believing that we led her to such happiness. All the while, our still, small voice continues to say, "This is a friendship brought together by us. Trust and enjoy."

To deal with one of your fears, you may want to take the

following actions:
- Ask us to give you clear guidance.
- Imagine the joy there could be.
- Bring it all to us in prayer. No worry is too small.
- When you know that to act is our will, be willing to push through the anxiety.
- You could pray the following:

Dear God,

There is more joy out there than what I am experiencing. Even though I know it's important to have a positive view of myself, I still have the painful thought that I am not good enough.

I am tired of being nervous around people I perceive to be better than me. I'm tired of being introspective. I'm tired of worrying. I'm just plain tired. I need a jump start. Help me see myself as your creation, a person worthy of love, of joy, of a good life. That is what I believe you want for all of us. You came to give us an abundant life. I'm just not living it right now. I don't even ask for a trouble-free life. I just ask to be so filled with you that the self-consciousness goes away. I'd like the truth that you are in my life to be a truth that will set me free. You seem to offer that. I accept.

Lord, I've got to move on in faith. I'd like to contact a certain person. My doing it would demonstrate that I believe I am worthy of someone else's time and consideration. Whether or not this person wants to talk with me is not even the issue. It is how I feel about myself. Help me see that someone would be lucky to get to know me, rather than just the other way around.

Help me take some action, today. Thanks for believing in me, especially when I don't. Amen.

How can I experience the feelings of my heart?

"WE" is God who is within you.

Is there such a thing as caring too much for someone? Is it wrong to want to have an equal amount of give-and-take? You may be familiar with the pain of unrequited love. There are also times when no one is keeping score, when you both have loving feelings of the heart. How can you experience more love and less pain in your partnerships?

Valerie and Ruth slowly developed a friendship that has lasted over three years and includes many good times and rich conversations. Valerie has also had some bad luck in relationships and has a nagging fear that something could go wrong at any time with this one. In fact, there's a part of Valerie that feels as if this is too good to be true. When Ruth was extremely occupied with family obligations she did not call Valerie for several days. Rather than ask what was going on, Valerie started to imagine that Ruth was just losing interest. In fact, she had almost convinced herself that Ruth didn't like her anymore.

When her life calmed down, Ruth asked Valerie if she wanted to go to the movies. Valerie dealt with her hurt by saying that she wasn't able to go. Ruth couldn't understand her friend's distance and was actually irritated by the whole thing. All of a sudden, this friendship was on rocky ground because of Valerie's insecurity. We want Valerie to see that as she realizes our love for her, she won't be as needy with her friends.

It is tempting to end a friendship when you don't get what you want. Of course, if it is an abusive situation, then you should break up. What we're talking about is when two people experience true feelings of love for one another. If yours is such a relationship, then don't end it. By closing your heart and saying, "I don't want to be your friend anymore," no one wins.

Sometimes it is right to end a union. Ask for our guidance in this decision. We will help you see if this is or could be a rich exchange of love, or if it is one-sided and unhealthy for you. Come to us and we will lead you to what is best for you.

Actions you could take:

- Relish the rich times you've had in the friendship.
- Recall why you are so happy to have him/her as a friend.
- With as open a heart as you can muster, ask for our guidance.
- Learn to give the gift of honest communication.
- If your heart tells you it is not a healthy relationship, ask us for the strength to end it.
- If you sense our encouragement to continue the friendship, then do so with joy.
- You may want to pray the following:

Dear God,

Thank you for the love and joy I feel when I'm with a good buddy.

Sometimes, when I am apart from a friend, my expectations become somewhat unrealistic. I want to be number one in this person's life. As time passes I let my imagination and insecurity take over. I figure my friend doesn't like me anymore because she hasn't called me within 24 hours of our last meeting. Lord, there seems to be a yearning in me that is crying to receive the attention that I am capable of giving others. When I find someone who is interested in me, I wonder if I scare that person away with my need for attention and reciprocity.

I am sorry if I expect too much. But, I don't want to go the other way either, giving too much.

I wonder if it would be easier if I stopped measuring who gave what last, and to whom. Help me learn to give my love freely, receive graciously and then let go. God, I don't have to be so insecure if I remember that I have your undivided attention. I do not have to share you with anyone. You exceed all my expectations. When I am trusting that you will meet my needs, I'll be easier on my friends. This will lessen the chance of my giving up because they don't love me enough. You do. And you are all I need. Amen.

Where have all the soul mates gone?

"WE" is God who is within you.

More time and energy are invested in finding and keeping a life partner than in just about anything else. In relationships there is disappointment as well as happiness.

Pat, Dennis, Joyce and Steve are each single and would like to have a significant other. Pat was in a serious relationship with a man for several years before he died of cancer. Now, she feels as if she has lost her chance and her charm. Dennis is getting frustrated because his partner seldom talks about how she feels. Dennis needs to know what he means to her. Joyce longs to be married and to have a child. Steve has been divorced for ten years. He remembers the good times and is more than ready to have that kind of intimate love and sharing again.

The sadness and longing are real. When people tell you, "It must be God's will for you to be single. The right person will come along at the perfect time," know that we can give you better comfort than that. In fact, these words can feel very hollow when you are lonely.

We know how discouraged you feel with the thought that it is our will for you to live your life alone. What is meant to be is your happiness. Period. Being single is not your cross to bear. Surely it is not our will that you agonize while others have a loving partner.

First, we want you to learn to love yourself, so that someone else can do the same! Are you disappointed with certain parts of who you are? These parts need love and acceptance. Do you say to yourself, "I should be happy, at least I've got my..." Hey, we want you to experience abundance in all aspects of your life. Oh and by the way, there's nothing wrong with using a dating service or a lucky charm, so don't feel guilty. No need to apologize.

In your attempts to find a new friend, just don't forget about us. Why? We understand you and know what is best for you. Can you surrender to our will? The part that you may not understand is that our will is good. Turning it over to us does not mean that you are giving up. This act of surrender will give you more freedom. In fact, it will make you more attractive. Your need will be gone.

Being in a personal relationship with us and learning to hear our voice will help you feel loved and complete. In the past, if you went to an event by yourself, you may have felt lonely. With acknowledgement that we are truly with you, you are no longer alone. You can even talk and laugh with us the next time you go solo to a concert.

Actions you may want to take:
- Dedicate yourself to being in a relationship with us.
- Have faith that we are in charge of your life.
- Acknowledge daily that we are your best friend.
- You may want to pray the following:

Dear God,

When I see a happy couple walking hand-in-hand, I am reminded of how much I want that in my life. I am tired of being invited to a wedding and seeing my name "and guest." I don't want just a guest, I want a life partner! I really don't care about a spiritual relationship with you. You can't hug me.

I want some touch, some words of love and care. How can you do this for me? I want to get a phone call from someone who is calling just to see how my day is going. I want to be special

24

to someone.

You say that you can actually be this person for me? Well, I am so tired of being lonely, that I will give this relationship with you another try. You know that I've talked with you before so this is not a new concept. The new part is the faith that you are asking me to have.

Help me see that I am loved by you at this very moment. Help me feel it. Help me realize that your love is deeper than any physical touch. This is hard for me to believe on one level. On another level, the knowing is what I'm really looking for. I can have this with you by faith. Help me hear your voice of love and care. Help me realize that you are ready to talk with me at any time of the day or night. Lord, be my first life partner. I'll trust you for the next one. Amen.

Needing to divorce but feeling afraid

"WE" is God who is within you.

We are with you when you marry. We are with you when you get divorced, too. How many of you are staying in your marriage for the sake of the kids? The instinct to be a good parent and the willingness to do anything for your children are blessings, usually. When it keeps you from facing your pain, a blessing becomes a curse. Hearing experts quote statistics on how children from "broken" homes have more problems than children whose parents stay together, makes the decision to separate almost impossible. You can make a choice for health and sanity, and sometimes this means divorce.

Candice and Richard were married for almost ten years. Candice had an exciting career and three daughters she spoke of with great love and pride. The fact that she didn't talk much about Richard, or that few of her friends knew him, didn't appear to matter that much because Candice seemed to be just fine. Then, she started to cry more easily and worry about being a bad mother. When their three-year-old daughter broke her arm while Candice was on a business trip, Richard didn't phone her until several days after it happened. Candice wondered, "Why didn't he call me right away? What did he tell my daughter? What does he tell the children about me when I'm gone?"

When Candice allowed herself to question her husband's motives, she was horrified with what she found. Suspicions she had had for years were confirmed. Richard told the girls that Mom didn't care as much about them as she did about her career. He often criticized his daughters and taught them to fear him. In her efforts to make sure that the girls didn't see Mom bad-mouth Dad, Candice pretended that all was well. Candice slowly came to the awareness that her daughters were hurt by their father, that she was abused by her husband, and that she needed to get a divorce. This kind of pain happens and we want to help. We helped give Candice the strength to get out of her marriage.

Candice had been quietly beaten down by Richard for years. She knew the relationship was not fulfilling. In her heart she was clear that living without a father would be better for the girls than living with him. However, she bought into what she thought the experts were saying. Her reaction was to ignore her inner voice and live with sadness and resignation. Furthermore, she needed to accentuate the positive in her work and as a mother, so she could even convince herself that it really wasn't that bad: "All marriages have problems. We have shelter, food and occasional love. It could be a lot worse."

Candice suffered in silence. She felt alone. Sometimes she felt crazy. "He must be a good man, I married him. People in the community tell me what a great teacher he is. The girls idolize their dad." Actually, the girls were confused, partially because Candice was telling them that everything was okay. The girls knew that all was not well, but if Mom said things were fine, well, Mom knows best.

When most of the headlines say that divorce will damage the children, that is what you could start to believe. Candice found almost a complete absence of research that supported her instincts. Although the articles didn't exactly say the following, all Candice could hear was, "Getting a divorce will hurt your kids. Children whose parents have divorced won't go to college and will not be able to have healthy relationships. You are a failure as a parent if you divorce."

Toward the end of the marriage, the lies and hurt that Richard was inflicting upon the family got so great that Candice had to insist that he move out of the house. Candice had always prayed and often heard our voice. The desire to do all for her precious daughters kept her in denial about how bad the marriage was. In desperation, she started to listen to our voice on this painful issue. She knew we wanted health and happiness for her family. Candice asked for help and found people who loved and supported her. Eventually Candice was able to divorce. The process was difficult. Now, on the other side, she is grateful. Her daughters are blossoming. The lack of tension in the home is heavenly. "When things aren't working, we talk about it rather than pretend that all is well."

Are you concerned about your marriage? Are you worried that your children will suffer more with divorce than if you stay married? Are you getting messages from authority figures that just don't ring true for you? There is no one right way. Sometimes we do lead you to divorce. We want the best for everyone.

We are not against experts. We just want you to know that you have a source of infinite wisdom inside you. No one will ever know you like we do. Do not doubt this power that is within you.

Actions to help you with your marriage:

- Meditate, pray and let us know you want our guidance. We are ready to help. We just don't want to barge in on you.
- Explore the nagging voice that tells you to do something that is contrary to what you believe to be the norm, or the "right thing."
- Honor your thoughts and feelings rather than deny them,

rather than call yourself stupid, rather than say, "I shouldn't feel this way."
• Know that you are a reflection of us and that we are in you.
• You may want to pray the following:

Dear God,

I look at what I've been through and now realize the incredible amount of stress I was living with. I was faithful and self-sacrificing. I did the very best that I could do at the time.

What happened? I forgot to honor someone even more important than my spouse. I forgot to love, cherish, listen to and honor myself. To listen to the still, small voice within me has been one of my lessons to learn and relearn.

For several years, I had a knowing and denied it. Why? There seemed to be too much at stake. Since my first child was born, I have always had such a strong maternal instinct. There's nothing I wouldn't do for my children. Nothing. They are my life. Sure, I enjoy my career. For me, though, work does not come close to the love that I have for my daughters. I denied the feelings that would lead me to disrupt the family, or so I thought.

As soon as I started to listen to your voice, clarity and synchronicity started to happen. You gave me faith in myself and in my thoughts. You brought old and new friends into my life who assisted me in making the decisions I needed to make.

I can't thank you enough. Now, my prayer is for those who are still out there suffering like I was. How can I help them deal with their loneliness and helplessness? I offer myself to you, Lord, to be a helper, to be a spokesperson, to be a friend and counselor. My heart is heavy for those who are hurting. Use me to help someone else see your light, to help someone else find a way out of feeling trapped.

Oh Lord, I need your help for one more thing. Help me work through my feelings toward my ex-husband. Show me the best ways to deal with the anger. If possible, help me be able to forgive and let go of my resentments. I want to do this so I can feel light, whole and free. If you are really capable of miracles, enable me to pray for him with compassion and wishes for his recovery.

Thank you, again, for helping me believe in myself, for helping me hear your voice. I dedicate my life to you. Help me be the best mother I can be to my children. Also, please help me continue to love, listen to and honor myself. Thank you. Amen.

section three

Career and Life Transition

I've got to get a job!

"WE" is God who is available to all.

For all of you who are gainfully employed, recall a time when you were out of work and looking for your next source of income. According to the world's standards, you are without identity or security. This can be a lonely and worrisome place. Could there be joy even in the search?

Larry graduated from law school almost three years ago. He has had some work projects, six months here, three months there, but he doesn't have a real job yet. He has loans to pay and friends to respond to when they ask, "How's the job search going?"

He's become depressed and hates to admit that food, sleep and TV are sometimes the highlights of his day. He fights with his thoughts, "Why should I get motivated and start networking again since it feels like I go one step forward and two steps backward? If I stop the forward motion, maybe the backsliding will stop too."

Larry is not alone, but when he's sitting in front of the TV finishing off a bag of chips, he feels pretty isolated. After overeating, staying up too late and knowing in retrospect how stupid that last TV show was, Larry doesn't want to get up at all the next morning.

There are times when making another networking call feels just too difficult. He is disappointed because this is so different from what his picture was: "A law degree, with a specialty in taxes —of course they'll want me!"

Hearing an executive search specialist say that he's not very hirable until he gets some job experience is enough to make him totally frustrated. "But, how and where do I get the experience that

33

they always seem to want?"

Larry is able to pull himself together and make more phone calls but wonders how long he can continue. These periods of depression seem as if they're getting longer and the networking is becoming more and more anxiety-provoking. "What if a time comes when I can no longer get myself up?" Larry's self-esteem slips a bit more each day.

Larry says that he's prayed enough and quite frankly doesn't see any results. We know he's disappointed in our seeming non-action.

Our timing is often different from your expectations. Let us offer a new perspective, not just for Larry, but for all of you who are feeling desperate to find work. You may want to take any of the following actions. Notice the special attention given to how you start and end your day.

- Invite us to be your co-job-hunters. Have a daily time of prayer and meditation in which you specifically ask for our help.
- End each day with us in a time of evaluation. Make sure this includes positive comments, even if all you did was read the want-ads.
- Before bed, draft a plan for the next day. Choose the clothes that you will put on when you start your day.
- Turn off the TV earlier than you used to, or don't even watch it. We'll help you get out of this rut. Sell it, put it in a closet, or give it away if you must!
- Right before bed, enjoy anything soothing such as a helpful book, music, yoga, meditation, exercise or a bath.
- Upon rising, envision us helping you stay focused. We will assist you in research and give you advice.

- Decrease your intake of caffeine, sweets, salt and fat. Increase the amount of water you drink. Add some moderate exercise to your routine.
- Treat getting a job as if it is your full-time job.
- Experiment with dressing up at home. Get out of your sweats. Make sure that you are well groomed every day.

We know it is hard. Asking for our partnership is your first step. We will help you continue the process of creating ideas and taking action each day. Lay down the burden of trying to do this all by yourself. You may want to pray the following:

Dear God,

Help! I feel so depressed about my lack of career success. This is not at all where I thought I'd be by now. Lately I've had to work very hard just to maintain a grown-up face, when what I really want to do is cry, or hit someone! I feel embarrassed, out of control and needy. Since I've gotten myself into this sad state, I'll be the first to admit, I'm coming to you, God, as sort of a last resort.

After graduation, I had confidence and didn't see a need to pray for help. Now, I've been knocked down. I've tried other ways and they haven't worked so you are my latest attempt at sanity and at getting a job. You'd probably be more complimented if I came to you out of want, not need. Sorry.

No apology needed, you say? You're just glad I'm asking for help? You're not going to hold it against me that I used to think I didn't really need you? Thanks! How gracious. This time of searching has become so disappointing that I am encouraged to have you on my team. In fact, I ask you to be the leader. I don't feel quite as alone with you. Please don't forget about me. I'll be needing, looking for and appreciating your help. In fact, if I can really start viewing this as a partnership, if I see myself teamed with the almighty, that just might give me some hope.

In fact, how can I lose when you are in control? This calls for a major attitude adjustment that may take me some time. We both have time, right? Great! Lord, help me see you as my partner. Let's go! Thank you. Amen.

I don't like my job

"WE" is God who is available to all.

Most of you have had a workday from hell: your boss is a grump, your computer crashes, you have to work late and miss your child's piano recital. A day like this is tolerable from time to time, but what if you had days like this all of the time?

The first two years of Alissa's job weren't that bad. In retrospect, it was a time when her talents were most valued and she was probably the happiest. Alissa even pictured herself staying with the company for many years. Then she got a new boss.

Autonomy was important to Alissa and her new boss was a micromanager. The boss took over the responsibility for all of Alissa's projects. The message to Alissa was clear, "You're not capable of making a decision without my approval. Every letter you write and idea you have must go through me." This style may work for some, but not for Alissa. She felt as if life was literally being sucked from her. Once an always-to-work-early kind of gal, Alissa wasn't even able to recognize who she was becoming. She looked for every possible excuse to get out of work. "What's happening to me? Do I have any talent or integrity left? Help!"

The easy solution for Alissa would have been to call her boss a jerk and complain daily, but who wins with this? Alissa asked to be transferred several times and the requests were denied. Finally, Alissa chose to leave.

How does this happen? When you get a new job you hope for the best. Sometimes you select your job from several offers. Other times you take the work because it was the only thing available.

Bad jobs happen.

Rick started to feel trapped in his work because in spite of the increases in pay and benefits, his job tasks became more unsatisfying. Rick was able to buy a home and provide for his spouse and daughter (which were his top priorities), but eventually, he felt like he was dragging himself to work. It was not quite at the "I hate my job" status, but almost.

Janet's employer was going through major changes and her benefits were better when she first started the job eight years ago than they are now. She doesn't even have a guaranteed number of work hours per week. She has less security than ever and less fulfillment.

When work is drudgery, you have an opportunity to curse us, leave us, or get closer to us. Your misery is our concern. We know the degree of your disgust and agony. Our help is available to you for the asking. Dealing with an unhappy work situation is not as hard when you have our guidance.

Actions you could take include the following:

- No matter how dismal things seem, affirm that nothing separates you from our abundant love.
- Immerse yourself in the thought, "God loves me, protects me and surrounds me. With God for me, who can be against me?"
- Keep up your faith. Start or increase the amount of time you spend in prayer and meditation.
- Do volunteer work to help you create a new perspective. You could choose a homeless shelter, a literacy program, a home for crack babies, or find another meaningful form of giving to those in need.
- You may want to pray the following:

Dear God,

I don't like my job. I don't like my boss. I'm not too fond of who I am becoming, either. I am so negative. I no longer have pride in my work. I've been late to work. I've bad-mouthed my co-workers. I've cheated my company out of time that was due. This is all because I feel so used and unappreciated.

I am just about as low on life and work as I've ever been. People who look forward to going to their jobs are the luckiest people in the world. My enthusiasm, drive and creativity are gone.

I have a faint memory of happier days. What I long for is the feeling of a job well done and a modest amount of recognition from a co-worker or supervisor. That would be heaven, a sip of water to someone dying of thirst.

I know this is a bit melodramatic, but I do have these times of drama. Don't get me wrong. I used to be a conscientious, industrious worker. It is just that now I feel so beaten down.

How long does it have to last? I'm sounding like I'd like you to swing from the rafters and rescue me from this mess. Oh yeah. I suppose I have some responsibility for getting here. What does that have to do with anything?

The only thing that is dawning on me is that if I got myself into this mess, then, perhaps I could get myself out. But, Lord, that is why I am praying, so that you will get me out. You know I've tried. What? How hard have I tried? Well, that is sort of a personal question, isn't it? I've been complaining about the job forever. Oh, that wasn't your question.

Lord, I'm coming to you for comfort and I feel like you're attacking me. OK, to get you off my back, I admit that I did apply for the job once upon a time. But I did not know it would turn out to be such a disaster. Whose side are you on, anyhow?

Back to my prayer, before I was so rudely interrupted. I'd like some help in getting out of this job. Lord, are you available to help me or not? Good. So, I am coming to you in prayer to... What is your nagging question? For some reason, it seems like you are wanting me to own my ability to do things, to say, "I'm not going to take it anymore."

Now, I'm getting the picture. If I don't do it, who will? Well, what do I need you for, then? I need you to help me help myself. I have forgotten that with you all things are possible. I actually used to believe that and somewhere along the line, I'm sorry, but I stopped.

I'd like to team up with you. I accept your spirit to lead me. Show me your will. I'm ready to try to make this job better or move on. I need your help. If you are for me, who can be against me? Thanks for being with me and being for me. Help me believe this, especially on the hard days at work. Give me hope that it can and will get better, okay? I'm trusting you. Amen.

How could they lay me off?

"WE" is God who is available to all.

Whether you complained about your job or loved it while you had it, one thing is for sure: life changes after this kind of involuntary career transition. We will help you make it through. Sometimes there is an uneasy feeling before a company downsizing. Other times, position endings can come out of the blue.

Ned worked in the training department for a mid-sized corporation. He was honest and hardworking. He figured that the company would treat him fairly and keep him employed until his retirement. When he heard that in order to save money, his organization would be encouraging certain employees to take early retirement with reduced benefits, he started to worry. When he was told to either apply for this early retirement or leave, Ned was shocked. "I've been giving my all. This is the thanks I get?"

Whatever the circumstances were that led to your sudden career ending, now is the time to look at where you get your security. The world tells you that security comes from income, insurance and investments. Where do you put your trust?

When income is unknown, people are more likely to come to us. We are not saying that we planned Ned's forced retirement so that he would become closer to us. What we are saying is that we can use it for good. Yeah, yeah, yeah, you've heard this before. Well, we do use hard times, if you let us. When life gets tough you can ask for our help or let go of your faith and say, "Why should I believe in God when this happened to me?"

To follow are some actions you may want to take which will

help you deal with employment uncertainty:
- Spend time daily in meditation and prayer.
- Ask us to help you release all of your negative feelings such as the shame of not having a job and the resentment toward those who were not laid off.
- Breathe deeply and be conscious of each inhale as a time when you are inviting us in.
- With your every exhale, see yourself breathing out all your anger, fear, worry and concern.
- Use this mindful breathing as a form of relaxation.
- Meditate on what you think our view of security is for you.
- Ask us to help you accept what happened and let it be. Live in the security of knowing that you are a child of the all-present, all-knowing, all-powerful God and that your needs are being taken care of.
- You may want to pray the following:

Dear God,

I just didn't think that this would happen to me. It doesn't seem fair. What did I do? I'd like to ask my boss, if you can help me get my courage up. I'd like to know if there was a reason that the company chose to let me go. What if I have a blind spot that I need to work on? I want to learn all I can to avoid this happening again. Sometimes these decisions are purely financial and not personal. I just want to find out for sure.

Lord, I still feel plugged-in about the whole thing. I don't like being resentful. It seems to take a toll on my health and energy. Show me how to let go of what I think should have happened. Help me let go of my expectations in general. Now that I'll be looking for new work, I need to be free from anything that could hold me back.

Life would be less stressful if I were able to take one day at a time and just thank you for what happens. I'd love to be able to live like this, with more freedom and less control. I will practice the idea that there truly is nothing that is sure in life other than the security you offer. I put my faith in you. Help me in my job search. I will look for my next job with new energy, knowing that you are with me. What an opportunity for me to see if I really mean it, huh? I believe, Lord. Help me with my unbelief. Amen.

I'm not yet ready for retirement

"WE" is God who is available to all.

Do you need to work a few more years before you retire? Or, have you already retired, but the word "retirement" is actually for someone else, not for you? Has it all come much too fast? As you journey into and through this life transition you may have periods of fear and regret as well as times of gratitude and joy.

Bev, 62, wishes she had a large savings account ready to provide her a monthly income. She wouldn't even mind finding an eligible and attractive person to help with these things. However, she is currently without the partner or the cash. So, she needs to find one more job before retirement. Bev made 20 interview appointments for a recent job hunting trip. She values her worth and has a dollar amount that she will not go under when job negotiating.

As Bev shares her ups, downs and hopes with us, she feels more connected and cared for. When she asks for help, we give her caring friends and energy to make the necessary follow-up phone calls.

We offer this type of support to you as well. We guide you with our still, small voice. We show you options. We help you to continue discovering, developing and using your unique gifts.

Bud, 63, retired from his last job, and was restless. "I am not ready to sit in a rocking chair, not ready for a very long time. I still have so much that I would like to contribute." Bud took the time to assess what he really wanted to do, and is now tired in the evenings, but happy. He does some work as a consulting engineer and built an airplane hangar as an investment project. "This will keep me occupied for years, and I love it! Best of all, I get to keep my own plane in the hangar!"

Sheri cannot believe that she turned 65 this year. She has so many things to do, that she could have easily retired from the working world yesterday. It's just that she needs to put more money into the nest egg before she starts to draw from it. At the same time, she also believes that there is more to life than money. Sheri let go of her higher-paying and stressful corporate job. She has now taken work with fewer hours per week and higher job satisfaction. "I can do this for several more years if the job description stays the same. If it changes for the worse, I'll look for something else. I'm grateful for today, and uncertain about tomorrow."

During career transition, you have several decisions to make. Call upon us to help you make the best choices so that you can enjoy your later years just as much or more than the earlier ones. Don't get sucked into believing that your life should become boring, dull, and dreary just because you are growing older.

When you find new gray hairs or when it takes you a bit longer to get out of bed, gracefully accept that everyone's physical shell starts to wear out after a time. It takes too much energy to fight these things. You know people of all ages who are living full, rich lives. Strive for this kind of beauty and joy, rather than for good looks.

And another thing, don't give up on love. We know how much you'd like to have intimacy and excitement. We want it for you, too. Keep an open mind toward all whom you meet. Sometimes the person who will touch your heart is not in the package you expected. Love may come to you through a new partner, friend, family member, senior citizen, young child or new baby.

Age comes. Come to us, and we will give you peace. Here are a few actions you could take that will help make the transition smoother:

- Increase your daily dialogue with us.
- Practice saying, "Thank you, Lord."
- Know that you can still have purpose and meaning in your life.
- Look for our intervention and our signs.
- You may want to pray the following:

Dear God,

Wasn't it just yesterday that I turned 40? Lord, how come it isn't like I dreamed it would be? I need some more money before I can even think of retiring. My perfect partner hasn't shown up yet, either. I have worked hard. Isn't it time for me to be able to relax? Isn't it time to feel fulfilled? To travel?

How can I make this transition as smooth as possible? How can I keep my good health? I'd rather not end up being dependent upon my family. When I start thinking of the future, I could worry. No wonder I try to avoid these kinds of thoughts.

Usually I have plenty of faith. It's just that I've got to talk with someone. I appreciate this chance to refresh your memory about me and my possible future needs. You don't need your memory refreshed? Great. As long as you know what I need, I should be okay.

The next time I get one of these waves of anxiety, I'm going to come to you faster than I used to. I'm going to trust that you do hold me in the palm of your hand and that you do care for my health and well being. Please help me make wise plans regarding my future.

Lord, I want you to be my number one form of happiness and security. I put my life in your hands. Amen.

Life after losing a spouse

"WE" is God who is available to all.

If you have lost your spouse of course the pain is great. The longer the time you spent together, the greater the transition will be for you to learn to live without your spouse and to possibly love again. Your life is not over. Take as much time to grieve as you need. Perhaps you can be encouraged by Barb's story.

Buddy and Barb were married for almost 40 years. They raised three children on the family farm and were just starting to have more time together as a semi-retired couple. Buddy discovered that he had cancer and the last five years of their marriage were filled with shock, hope, sadness and lastly, acceptance that Bud would die.

From the day of diagnosis, time became more precious for Bud and Barb. Committed to the marriage, Barb never once doubted her decision to see Bud through and be as loving and supportive as possible. As his cancer progressed, Barb's role of wife, nurse and caretaker became more exhausting. Her grieving started long before Buddy died.

Of course Barb's first choice was to grow old with her husband. When this did not happen, she realized that, at age 58, she had almost half of her life left to live. Through the ups and downs of married life, raising kids, and just plain living, Barb's faith grew strong. She knew that she could count on us to help her deal with this major life change.

Married at age 19, Barb now had a whole new life to live as a single person. Once Bud died, she started to do things she had never done before such as attending a semester of college. She found a job working outside the home as an office manager for a used car dealership. She traveled with friends and redecorated her home. Giving special love and care to her children and grandchildren became even more important to her than ever before.

Four years after Buddy died, an old friend of Bud's (whose wife died of cancer, also) asked Barb out for a date. They were married within months. Barb is grateful for all of her life, the married and the single years.

How about you? You surely do not have to remarry to enjoy your life. What we want you to know is that no matter how deep your loss, nothing will ever separate you from our love. We want you to let go enough so that you can start to live again. How? Barb did it through her daily quiet time of prayer and devotion. She asked us for guidance. We led her to new and rewarding friendships. We showed Barb ways to lend a helping hand and give a listening ear to those in need.

We will also help you get on with your life. We're with you through your grieving and we will help you gradually come out of the sadness.

Actions you could take:
- Invite us to be with you in this new stage of your life.
- Slowly let go of your spouse by releasing him or her into our capable keeping.
- When you are ready, give or sell some of your partner's possessions to family, friends or charity.
- If you need to, move out of the home where you shared so many memories.
- Ask friends to give you specific support, such as phone calls, dinner, walking dates or even private time.

- Be gentle with yourself, especially when you are trying something new.
- You may want to pray the following:

Dear God,

Half of my life is gone now that my spouse has passed away. I know there could still be a full life for me, but a part of me wants to leave, too.

I need help in how to deal with this. I trust that there is a path and purpose for me now. Help me see it. I'm afraid that I may need to grieve for quite a while. When it is time for me to make some changes, that will be difficult, too.

I can't decide now, but someday, I'll need your guidance in what to do, where to live, what to keep, what to sell and what to give away. It is all so overwhelming for me.

I want companionship. Lead me to the people who have love for me. I'm open to form new friendships or rediscover some of the people who have been in my life all along. I just feel scared. I'm such a newcomer to the single life. I don't want to deal with this by myself. Thank you for the family and friends who care about me. I want your spiritual help, too. I want all the help I can get.

Also, I'm afraid that I may make some mistakes. Help me be kind to myself. There are probably not too many things that I could really muck up that badly, are there?

I know you are with me. Be my guide. Be my comfort. Be my rest. Thank you. Amen.

Getting older

"WE" is God who is available to all.

As your parents grow older they will need more care. How can you deal with the pain and maximize the possibilities for joy?

Joe's 82-year-old father, Harry, came for a four-week visit. Now in a wheelchair, Harry needed more help getting around. After ten days of being together, Joe wanted some time alone. Harry started to feel like he was imposing and worried that he had worn out his welcome.

Joe was used to a certain lifestyle which became disrupted. Joe thought to himself, "I should be willing to do anything for him because he's my father. Look at all he has done for me. But, I'm tired of this."

During these times of disappointment, we are ready to give relief. We can make this situation not only tolerable, we can make it a positive experience. Ask for our help.

Is there any way that you could receive from the person to whom you are giving care? This would make the magical difference for both of you. Harry loves to be helpful. Joe felt silly at first, but asked his dad to repair a leaky faucet. Harry felt useful, the dripping stopped, and they both smiled.

Harry lived through the Depression. Joe decided to learn about that period of history from him. Joe also asked his dad to describe details about his growing up. Harry was pleased to know that he was telling his son something he enjoyed.

If you are taking care of an elderly person (even if only for a few days):

- Know that you are in need of special self-care when you are caregiving.
- If you are burned out, look, ask, even beg for help. Many of you are too stubborn or proud to ask.

If you are the recipient:

- Know that sometimes it is easier to give than to receive care.
- Practice being a gracious receiver.

Prayer for those who spend time giving care:

Dear God,

I'm humbled when I think of the level of love and care some are giving to others. I could never do it. What's wrong with me? I can hardly handle a couple of weeks. At least I have the will to change. In fact, this morning, I was quite loving for a few hours and I like myself better when the love is flowing. Later today, I was rude because I had something important to work on. I didn't want to have to interrupt my plans just to help my dad.

Please give me your love. That is what it is all about, isn't it? When he leaves at the end of his trip, I want to feel good about the visit (especially if it is the last time I see him, which it could be). Help me get the right perspective. I know that you would never give me more than I can handle.

Lord, sometimes I can be an excellent listener, a pleasant companion and a great hand-holder. I like myself when I am filled with your love. Help me see that you can make our time together much more loving when I ask for your help. Actually, when I think of the unconditional love I've received from family and friends, then I realize that I *want* to pass it on. Amen.

Prayer for those who are aging:

Dear God,

All my life I have been the caregiver. I gave so much to my parents, my spouse, my children, my grandchildren and my neighbors. To be a giver is a comfortable lifestyle I've come to love.

Now, what is this? Me being dependent upon others? Do I really need someone to be with me just to go outside? I'd rather take a tumble than be cooped up inside all the time. Well, no, I don't want to hurt myself, but you know what I mean. I'm having trouble realizing that my body is aging. I miss having the energy that I used to enjoy.

Truthfully, I want quality time with my son. I don't expect it to be perfect, because we've always had our moments. I just want to contribute to his happiness, not detract! Actually, it doesn't feel fair. I gave my best for him while he was growing up. Now, I am aging. He is trying to care for me. I don't think he's doing as good a job as I did for him! Do I want him to feel guilty? No. I just need someone to confide in so that I can get my love reserves restored. Lord, will you be my confidant? I know you are and can't thank you enough.

The bottom line is that we love each other. Help me show it. Melt the irritation we both feel. Help us see the big picture. Thanks, Lord. I'm counting on your help. Amen.

section four

Condemnation

Did I deserve this?

"WE" is the plural energy of God.

The idea that we are a God of punishment is so ingrained in some that whenever something goes wrong, the first reaction is, "I must have sinned and God is doing this to me." Let's look at Theresa.

Theresa and Gus had been married for several years and decided they wanted to have a baby. When Theresa found out that she was pregnant, both she and Gus were thrilled. Several months into the pregnancy, Theresa miscarried. She could not shrug off the thought, "God caused it. I deserved this misfortune because of a sin I committed against God."

Adults who were taught as children that God is punitive have a difficult time letting go of this notion. We are so sad that people are suffering needlessly with a false view of who we are.

Loss and hardship are difficult enough. Add the feeling of being convicted by God of some sin, and it is no wonder that people turn their backs on having any kind of a relationship with us.

How about you? Do you feel as if your problem is a result of our wrath? We weep for those of you who see us as that kind of a God. Please let us help you believe that we are a loving God, rather than one who is ready to hurt certain people who "deserve" to be punished.

To teach the concept that God punishes sinners is an injustice done to millions of people. The notion of God as unconditional love and kindness is foreign to many. Take a moment to look at the recipients of sickness, disaster and loss. Please notice that bad things happen to all people. Suffering is not intended to be retribution for sinners.

How can years of such programming be erased? There are usually no shortcuts. We do have some actions you can take that will help you in your healing:

- Imagine that we are unconditional love. See that we love you and did not cause your problem as a punishment.
- Notice how it feels to believe in a loving God.
- Increase or start having meditation time.
- Seek to hear our voice and to know our loving presence.
- You could pray the following:

Dear God,

Who are you, anyway? Are there times when you use your power to hurt others?

I am amazed at how strong this notion of God is in my life and I don't like it. I have been told that I did not deserve what happened to me, and that it was not a punishment from you. I want to believe this, and yet, it feels as if there is a demon in me that hangs on to the idea, "I deserve this because of my sin against God."

How can I break free from these thoughts? In my heart, I yearn to see you as a God of love. It feels right to view you as non-judgmental. Help me nurture this view.

My upbringing was confusing. At times, I did hear about the love of God. I heard that I should be loving to others. I believe in helping those less fortunate. Not all of my training was harmful, but some of it has turned me off to believing in any kind of a God.

Even so, I'd like to have a spiritual life. If I could see you as a loving, supreme being, as one I can turn to, one I can pray to, then I'd like to have contact with you. I could have used this kind of a God for comfort when my loss happened.

Lord, transform my mind, please. Help me develop a new faith in you, a loving God. Amen.

Going to the abortion clinic

"WE" is the plural energy of God.

When the circumstances that cause a pregnancy are not the best for bringing a child into the world, there is pain. A few comments from women who discovered that they were pregnant: "An abusive person forced me to have sex with him. I can't have a baby from this violation." "My brother made me pregnant and I'm only twelve years old." "I choose not to have this baby for very personal reasons."

Sandy agonized about what to do. She prayed to us for guidance. She weighed the pros and cons. She would have loved to have a child, but not at this time. In the quiet of her heart, we gave her peace about this decision. We did not condemn her for having sex. We were with her in her choice to have an abortion.

Sandy was not prepared for what happened next. She selected a clinic that was known for providing safe abortions. The day she went, there was a protest. As Sandy walked into the office, she heard people yelling, "Baby killer! God will punish you for the murder you are about to commit!"

All Sandy could think about was that she had an inner peace about her decision. Then, these protesters told Sandy that she was wrong, that she was a sinner.

Our main concern is for Sandy. What will she do now? What do you do when someone says that you have sinned and that God is going to punish you? You could let go of any kind of spirituality, stop believing in God, or become angry with God. This is where we have much to say.

You may wonder if we have feelings. We do. Our heart breaks

for Sandy and for those of you who have been told that we want to condemn you. This is not who we are. We are unconditional love. For example, if you squandered all your life savings on lavish living, denounced us, and then returned, wanting to start a new life with us, we would welcome you back with open arms. This is who we are.

Whenever someone says that God is angry with you, listen to our voice within you, rather than the blaming words of that person. Even when people seem certain about their rightness, come to us for your answers.

We cannot be anything but love. Our perfect love casts out fear. We give a peace that passes all understanding. Nothing will ever separate you from our love.

Next time you are condemned for an action, you may want to do any one of the following:

- Take Christ's words and make them your own, "Father, forgive them for they know not what they do."
- Envision our love surrounding you, so that their words will not hurt you.
- Spend extra time in meditation. Let us know if you are confused. Be as open as you can be. Pray for the knowledge of our will. Make your choices based on this time of quiet prayer.
- After prayer and meditation, take the answer you get and know it is from us.
- Seek fellowship and support from others who view us as a loving God.
- You may want to pray the following:

Dear God,

I would not have gone through with this if I didn't feel it was the best thing. How do I deal with these people who want to judge me?

There was such hatred in several of the protesters. They spoke of a condemning God, and they came to condemn me and the clinic staff. I talked with one who said that I could be spared from hell if I would just confess my sin. She was so righteous about her view that I wasn't sure I wanted forgiveness from the God she spoke of.

What will help me get through this is to know that you have not left me. I cannot believe that you are far off, angry with me for committing a sin. I can't imagine that all you need is my confession, and then you will come back to me. This just doesn't fit my picture of a loving God.

I dream about being a mother someday. If I do have a baby, I will tell this child about you, a God who did not give up on me. Lord, you are someone I want to share with my children. I'm not always sure who you are, but I really need to feel you in my life. Help me use this time to get closer to you, rather than farther away. Amen.

What will happen if
I do not accept Jesus?

"WE" is the plural energy of God.

Some people have the belief that accepting Jesus Christ as personal lord and savior is the only way to eternal life. In fact, Jesus says so himself in the Bible, "I am the way, truth and the life." Is there truly only one way to heaven? We want to minister to those of you who have agonized about this. Read about these children.

Lynn's two little girls were playing with their cousin, Marie. "You have to ask Jesus to come into your heart or else you are going to hell," blurted out Marie, the ten-year-old cousin. When the young girls came home to tell their mother, they were very worried. "Mom, why haven't we accepted Jesus? We better do it!" Then there was Tim who came home from school one day crying, "Dad, someone told me that since I am Jewish, I won't be going to heaven. Is that true?"

Marie's parents feel that the ultimate gift they could give anyone is an introduction to Christ. Marie knows how important this is to her folks and to her Sunday School teacher. So far, the intentions of everyone are positive. Something serious happens however, when the little girls hear that they will go to hell, when Tim hears that because of his Jewish faith, he does not have the beliefs that will enable him to go to heaven.

Our main concern is for those of you who feel alienated from us because of such messages. This kind of ultimatum leaves you with two options: believe and follow the heaven prescription; or, do not believe in it and be viewed as a sinner going to hell by those who do. We are more loving than that. We are bigger than any one religion.

If you have been told that you are going to hell because your beliefs are not quite right, come to us. Let us remind you that there are many views about us held by people from all over the world. Some choose to believe that there is only one way to inherit eternal life. Some of these people are filled with our love so that you will feel blessed by being with them. They know that love is the key.

It is you who we are worried about. If you are having trouble with one prescription and therefore are tempted to let go of any form of spirituality, or if you are feeling separate, guilty, and unsure of which way to go, just don't leave us! We are a God of love and acceptance. Throughout the ages, people have come to us. We've been called many names including God. What we are called does not matter. What does matter is that you are connected with us so that you can experience our joy, love and security, so that we can love others through you.

Some actions you could take that will help you:

- Identify any pain you have experienced based on your beliefs about God. Have you ever been told that you are going to hell? If so, write or talk with someone about your anger, frustration, sadness, disappointment or hurt.
- Write as if you could hear our voice. What would we tell you about us? What would we say about Jesus?
- Imagine having a loving spirit in your life that is all-knowing, all-loving, all-caring, a spirit that created you, knows you and loves you. What kind of a relationship would you like to have with this spirit?
- Find people and/or a place where you feel that your relationship with us is honored, nurtured and encouraged.
- You may want to pray the following:

Dear God,

Could it be that I do not have to subscribe to one certain belief to be right with you? I have known that there must be a divine spirit guiding me. It's when I'm told that you have a certain name, and only that name, that I get confused. I see the world as too big a place, and I see you as too big a God to let only a select few "in." I'm not even sure what heaven is. Maybe heaven is now!

Anyway, I am tired of feeling separate from you. I want a relationship so that I can ask for your help. I want to have a God to come to not only when I am in need, but also when good things happen. When I look at a beautiful sunset, I'd like to acknowledge, thank and be close to its creator.

I do not have it all figured out. Maybe I never will. I know that I was created to be in relationships with fellow humans and yet, I feel a void in my heart that can be filled by only you. Please don't fail me now. Show me signs of your presence. Open my eyes so I can see you in my life. If you are real, please give me a feeling of connection and a sense of wholeness.

I don't quite know what it means to dedicate my life to you. I'd like to try that too. I'd like to surrender my will to yours. I have a sense that your will is for my good. I know that you will not always shield me from problems. I also know that you will never leave me. That is what I want: to feel your presence. Since trials do and will come, I don't want to deal with them alone. I want what I've heard others talk about: peace that passes all understanding. I want you to be in my life, to be leading my life. I don't know how to do it, but I trust that you will show me. I'm counting on it. I'm counting on you! Amen.

Why do they call me a faggot?

"WE" is the plural energy of God.

Names like "faggot," "fairy," and "queer" are still being used. The pain can be great. How do you get beyond it?

Ever since Jeremy can recall, he knew his sexual preference was different from most of his other guy friends. It's hard enough getting through junior and senior high school with heterosexual preferences. Jeremy grew up being called disparaging names. The church his parents sometimes attended tried to be loving. But, to say that there is love for the sinner, not the sin, just didn't feel very loving to Jeremy.

To be called "fatso," "stupid," "dumb," "ugly," or "faggot," hurts. When people give you names like this, you are being verbally abused. You are receiving a communication that comes from ignorance, inferiority and/or hatred. Please come to us for comfort. The dilemma is that some of the name-callers are doing it in "God's" name from "God's Word."

How do you deal with getting comfort from us when you hear that we are not loving? Listen to our still, small voice inside your heart, rather than to the words of others said with judgment.

You can sometimes tolerate it if the ridiculing person is someone you don't really know or like. How do you deal with someone you care about who is condemning of homosexual preferences?

Please don't turn your back on us. We love you. We created you. See yourself in our image, that of creator, God. For your peace of mind, and for your ability to enjoy life, you may want to have a plan ready to activate if you are criticized. We wish that name-calling was over. We wish that all churches preached about love and acceptance such as Christ demonstrated, but this is not yet the case.

The following are some actions you might take the next time someone addresses you with an insulting name:

- Remember Jesus's words, "Father, forgive them for they know not what they do."
- Feel our love so totally encompassing you that their words do not hurt you.
- Say, "I'm sorry that you feel this way. I extend God's love to you in return."
- Exhale the sadness, hurt and anger you feel.
- Ask that we replace these feelings with our love, peace and joy.
- You may want to pray the following:

Dear God,

When I encounter hatred of homosexual behavior, I sometimes go into a panic. I wonder if I am cursed. When I listen to your still, small voice, I know I am loved by you. I know you created me just as I am.

What is really hard is that I love to worship you publicly. It seems as if I need to become aware of safe places to attend services. My first tendency is to label the place either homofriendly or homophobic. I'm tired of having to be so careful. Why do I have to deal with this at all? Well, I do. Since some people's views probably won't change, I want to choose the most loving response. Fighting back takes too much energy.

My dream is that we could all worship together. I want to be part of the solution of love, rather than part of any problem of separatism or exclusivity. On that note, Lord, are there any groups that I am discriminating against? Could it be that I have a blind area where I am doing the same thing? If so, please show me. I want to be a vessel of your unconditional love. I want to be like Christ. When others were crucifying him, he was able to have loving forgiveness. Could I use their scorn as an opportunity for me to speak of your love?

Maybe I can't on my own, but with you all things are possible. I do not want to be living in fear. I want to live in your freedom of love. Help me see that there is nothing that I can't handle with your spirit dwelling in me. I love having you teach me how to love. I gladly trust you with my life. Thanks for helping me do what I couldn't do on my own. Hallelujah! Amen.

Misunderstood

"WE" is the plural energy of God.

You know the feeling of having a friend upset with something she thought you said or did. It is joyous when miscommunication gets cleared up. It can be incredibly painful when it doesn't. Years of friendship have been thrown away due to nothing more than a misreading of someone else's actions. Let's look at Tara.

Tara has been a faithful Christian almost all her life. It is her profession to write and sing songs to glorify us. In the first half of her singing career the lyrics were all Christian. Tara started to receive our guidance to sing to a larger audience. Her last several projects included songs of love and life with little or no direct mention of us. The music packaging changed to attract the person who would never set foot in a Christian music store. Tara received some criticism from strangers and expected that. What she wasn't prepared for was the letter she got from a longtime friend, Sheila. In it, Tara was being accused of letting us down, letting Jesus down, and actually leading men to lust after her. Tara felt so misunderstood. "If my friend really knew me, she would never make this kind of an attack."

Sheila was taught that Christians should act, dress and sing in a certain way. Amazingly, people will hold on to beliefs about us more tightly than they will hold on to us! When you go against an established set of rules, you may lose some of your friends who are tied to those rules. This is what happened with Sheila and Tara.

Have you ever received a letter like the one Sheila wrote? Have you ever been scolded for not attending worship services? Have you ever been reprimanded for not doing it the right way? Have you been criticized for being of the world, not just in it? Maybe you needed the scrutiny. The issue here is being chastised for actions that we led you to take.

Your response can be a witness to our love. Recall how you made the choices that are now being judged. In Tara's case, she remembers praying over what to wear, what songs to record and how to advertise. She felt led by us to make certain choices. When you know that you have been following our leading, you feel our peace. As you breathe deeply, our love will flood back into your wounded heart, enough love for yourself and for your accusers.

If you have been misunderstood, here are a few actions you can take:

- Be like Christ and forgive.
- Let us refill, renew and nourish your spirit.
- Ask us to help you respond to the one who judged you.
- You may want to pray the following prayer, and feel free to change the words to make it your own:

Dear God,

What happened? Why doesn't my friend trust me? You know my heart. In one of my photographs, I have a tee shirt on that shows my body. The next thing I know, people are calling me a temptress. I quit!

Of course I don't quit. I love my music career. I love my spouse, family and friends. The opportunities you have given me to sing your praises have been unbelievable. I wake up daily thanking you for my life.

It's just that right now I feel attacked by a good friend who says that she is doing it out of love and concern. I don't think so. Well, she does seem sincerely concerned. It's her judgmental "rightness" and her apparent non-trust in our relationship that hurts.

There seem to be several options. I could tell my friend that she is right, I am wrong, and I will never do anything worldly again. I could tell her to drop dead. I could ignore her criticism. Dear Lord, there must be something else I could do. I know you will help me deal with this in the best, most loving way.

I also know that the only person I can change is me. I am sorry that my friend feels offended. It's not my nature to hurt anyone. In the next few days and weeks, I will meditate on how to best respond to her. I've received other letters, too, so I know that this criticism of me is out there. I have no desire to throw stones back at them. What I'd really like to do takes more love than I've got.

That's why I've been with you, Lord, since I can remember. You give us love that we would otherwise not have. I trust that you will continue to use me and show me your solution. Thank you for the blessing of having a career where I get to sing and speak of your love. Help me deal with this problem in a way that glorifies you and brings us all closer to you. I need your help and I know you are leading me. Hallelujah! I continue to joyfully sing your praises. Amen.

section five

Addiction and Recovery

Ninety days clean and sober

"WE" is God who is available to all.

Addiction. Some of you know first-hand what it is. Others of you know it because of someone you care about. The road of recovery has curves, hills, valleys and even a few mountain tops. No matter if you are starting on this journey for the first time, or fiftieth, it is "one day at a time" by our grace.

Kelly used alcohol and marijuana in high school, especially during the time when her parents split up. While in her twenties, she started to think that maybe this wasn't just a recreational sport. But it never seemed to be that bad. She always had a job and was able to pay for her living expenses most of the time. When she was up and feeling well, her hotel sales and marketing career would soar. When she felt depressed, she would usually indulge. After Kelly turned 30 she decided she would be better off not using.

For several years, Kelly would go on and off. She said she wanted to quit. She would quit for a while. Then she would use. She developed friends in the fellowship who cared for her and they started to lovingly lean on her, "When are you going to get it?" When funding became available for her to attend a treatment program, Kelly said "yes." During the treatment, once again, Kelly decided that she needed to stay clean and sober for her life to work. Today is Day 90, clean and sober.

It doesn't matter if Kelly inherited her affliction or got it all by herself. What matters is that we offer our help to Kelly and to all of you struggling with any kind of addiction. You could be addicted to cigarettes, alcohol, drugs, sex, TV, gambling, food or clothes. When your choices are driven by self-destructive behavior, when you regret what you've done, when you know that this is bigger than you are, then it's time to turn to us. Sure, we'd like it if you turned to us when your life was going well! But, whatever it takes, we are here for you.

We know the despair of wondering if you'll ever make it. We know how low you can feel about yourself. Nothing will ever separate you from our love. If you are waiting to have Day 1, or 100 or 1,000, we are always with you. We are your strength to stay clean and sober, one day at a time.

You may be involved with some sort of program to help you with sobriety. We encourage any kind of a spiritual routine that supports you in believing that we are at the heart of your wellness. We are present and ready to help. You may not hear our voice. Do not let that make you think we are absent. Talk with us often. Tell us about your ups and downs. Practice having faith without seeing the answers.

Find someone else who believes in us. Pray together, asking not only for our help, but also ask for our will to be done. Other actions you may want to take:

- Be with people who support your sobriety, people who believe in you.
- Learn to identify your vulnerable times and ask for help. It might be better for you to feel needy than to feel cocky.
- Adapt the, "There, but for the grace of God, go I" attitude.
- Help others who are in recovery.
- Envision that we help you be your best as you entrust your life to us.
- You may want to pray the following:

Dear God,

Today I have ninety days clean and sober. You know how many years I've been battling with this. You also know that I'm not always sure I have to live a sober life. It's just that this time things got really depressing for me.

Thank you for my sponsor. Thank you for the treatment program I just finished. And, now, thank you for the 90 days! I am grateful on many levels. Today, however, I don't feel it. I'm not necessarily happy. Actually, I'm rather grumpy, sad and fearful. I have some feelings that I don't even understand. In the past, if I had some marijuana, these feelings would pass.

Now, I feel everything. I am raw, out there and vulnerable. This is foreign and scary; however, there is a part of me that likes being so real. Help me get in touch with this small part so that it can grow.

I like letting my feelings be all right. I like the idea of waking up and knowing that I did not get stoned the night before. For today, my highest goal is to be clean and sober, one minute, one hour at a time. I'm sort of embarrassed that I have to have this as a goal. Couldn't it be a bit more lofty?

Of course, I can have other goals, too. Without being clean and sober, I've learned that nothing else works. Sobriety takes humility. I feel humbled. I also feel angry. How come I have to deal with this? My sister seems to be able to have a substance, enjoy it, and then go weeks without any white knuckles. She doesn't have the need or the craving I have. If I got the gene for chemical dependency and she didn't, that is really unfair.

Lord, still there? I know I'm complaining. But, I want to stay close to you. Part of my program is to maintain some form of prayer and meditation. I'd like the relationship with you to be real, up close and personal. I have a sense that there is nothing you haven't heard before. I bet that you can handle anything. Is it okay if I have these notions about you? It feels good to be able to talk with you as if you were a real person. If this is a spiritual program, if this is a feelings disease, then I need to feel you.

Also, I know you are holy and awesome. On that note, I need your help. What concept of you do you want me to have? How do you want me to talk with you? Some say that we shouldn't be too chummy with you because, after all, you are God. I wouldn't want to offend you. You are the spirit that will empower me to stay clean and sober, one day at a time.

I will answer a bit of the question I just asked. I bet it honors you when we talk freely and when I feel as if I can mention anything to you. If I acted like there were certain taboo subjects; that doesn't feel like real intimacy. I don't think I'd grow as much in my faith if I had to avoid certain topics. It would probably be those very issues where I most need you and your input.

I love being in a relationship with you. I don't see you as a physical, male, father figure. I see you as a being of great love, great power and great wisdom. I want to believe that you care about me. This is as awesome as it gets as far as I'm concerned. Now here's a question for you.

It is my 90th day. I want to be clean and sober, one day at a time, by your grace, for the rest of my life. Can I always call on you? If I am tempted to give it all up for one smoke, will you help?

Will you stop me from that first and fatal puff or drink? Will you help me help myself? I am coming to believe that a power greater than myself will help me. That power is you. I believe. Please help me when my doubts start to surface. Amen.

Sixteen years of sobriety

"WE" is God who is available to all.

At 52, Paul wonders why he is still having such a hard time handling his career and economic responsibilities. He's had a roller coaster of a ride in life. In his 16th year of sobriety, he's been told that getting financial affairs in order is often one of the last things to happen in the recovery process.

Paul has been seeking wealth with more passion and determination than most. He asks, "Why haven't my efforts been rewarded? What lesson haven't I yet learned?" Paul feels disappointed, discouraged and tired. Yet, he knows of no other way than to keep on trying, one day at a time.

Do you have a nagging dissatisfaction with your income? Are you trying to figure out how to build your savings account? Would you prefer not to borrow money anymore, even though you continue to make new debts? Is your spirit willing, but your flesh weak?

Refresh your memory of who we are. We are the King of Kings and Lord of Lords. Focus on our richness.

Somewhere along the way you stopped believing in our willingness to provide for you. All you notice is evidence to the contrary. We love you very much. We have blessed you with many talents. Unfortunately, there are still some lessons for you to learn. We are with you with each step. We know it seems like a very long process.

When you meditate, you wish that you heard us more directly. In your heart and mind, you do know our voice. It is time for you to let go of the world's definition of success and start seeing ours.

We have abundance for you materially. But first, surrender your desperate need. This need you have has an underlying message that is hurting you. The message is, "I am not okay until I have achieved a great deal of financial success." You are whole and complete because you are our child. Period.

In your heart, you know that we are the definition of success. You cannot take your possessions with you when you pass on. Grow in your need for us. Practice seeing yourself delighted in us and in us alone.

Here are some actions you may want to take:
- Start having or increase the time you spend in prayer and meditation.
- List and be grateful for all the gifts you have, including your 16 years of sobriety.
- Share these gifts with others.
- Let go of your fear of sponsoring someone new. We want to use you to bless others.

We know that you feel stagnant and sometimes paralyzed. Let us teach you the lessons. Let us give you a new life. Surrender your need to know how we're going to do it. Just be ready, willing and open! You may want to pray the following:

Dear Lord,

I have so many dreams yet to fulfill. I want to do much more traveling. At times I feel as if I've done everything humanly possible to try to figure myself out and that I'm just not curable. I sure hope that I don't give up.

I am disappointed in the results that you have given me. I've been faithful and why don't I have more to show for it? Overall, I have dedicated my life to you. You owe me, Lord! Of course, I'm kidding. I know that you don't owe me anything. Well, then, life owes me. Doesn't someone or something owe me? I've been on this planet for 52 years. I've been kind to strangers. I've been unkind too, but who's looking? I am good to my parents. I am loving to my spouse, at least most of the time. I want a good life. I want financial success. I want to be able to pay my bills, debts, taxes and support my family.

Lord, I want, I want, I want! Yet my goals are becoming more and more out of reach. Help me get out of this rut. On good days, I do see all that I have. Help me feel more gratitude for my blessings. I surely do not want to lose these out of my desperate need to get all of the other stuff that I think I must have.

I need a dependable monthly income so that there is less stress on myself and on those I love. But, how low do I have to go? Certain kinds of work feel beneath me, and you wouldn't want that for me, would you? You'd prefer that I use my gifts, right?

I don't know what you want. I do know what I want, and it's not happening! Do you have any encouragement for me?

You want me to listen daily for your voice? I've already tried and I told you, I don't hear anything. What? Are you saying that there is a part of me that is afraid to hear what you have to say? I give up that fear right now.

I surrender, again. Please show and tell me your will. I trust that you love me and have a plan for my life. I'm open, ready and willing to hear your voice. Gosh, Lord, I'd even work at a fast food place, if I knew it was your will. I'm counting on this not to be the case, but I'd do it. Your will be done. Thank you. Amen.

I can't stop eating

"WE" is God who is available to all.

Some of you who have been consuming food moderately all of your life have no idea that for others it is a daily battle of trying to eat in a healthy way. For those of you who have this struggle, we have come to bring you life and sanity.

Angie loves to eat. But this time it feels so out of control. "I've decided that it is too hard right now, and I'm just not going to worry about it." But, Angie does worry. She is sad that something so seemingly handleable has become extremely difficult to manage. When she looks into the mirror, she recalls slimmer days, and feels disappointed. Her life seems to be filled with other unknowns too, and this adds to her fear. "Will I ever be able to get this eating thing dealt with? God, where are you, anyway? I ask for help, and the help just doesn't seem to come."

Angie is not alone. Many of you have the same hopeless feeling. You wonder why it is easy for some and totally impossible for others. Please remember that with mankind, many things are impossible, but nothing is too hard for us. We know that this sounds trite. You feel like giving up because you cannot see any positive results. Please do not lose your faith in our healing power. It feels like the out-of-control eating is the thorn in your side. But you know that this is just a symptom. What is so painful that even eating too much and feeling miserable have less pain than the things that are really bothering you?

You have self-hatred that is hurting your soul. We want you to get to the bottom of your sadness. Are you willing to do whatever it takes to feel?

This is your life. We came that you might have life and have it more abundantly. Your suffering can stop. There is deep pain that you are not even aware of. Nothing is too scary when we are with you, and this truth will set you free. Write about your feelings. Have notebooks in the kitchen, in the car and at your workplace. Explore the anguish you have buried. We will help you take the necessary actions which may include the following:

- Write and tell us how you feel about yourself and your relationship with us.
- Right before you are about to overeat, take a deep breath, pray to us, and we will help you write instead of eat.
- Practice patience and perseverance. Know that we're with you every step of the way in your discovery and in your recovery.
- You may want to pray the following:

Dear God,

I know you are here for me. It's just that I've already asked for your help a zillion times. Yes, sometimes I do feel your strength. Other times, I hate to admit it but, I'd rather eat. In my most sober moments, of course I want your peace and freedom. The good news is that I know you will never give up on me.

Okay, I'll explore my pain. After an eating binge I mainly feel disgust and remorse about the eating. These feelings are so strong that I haven't noticed what other emotions may be leading me to overeat in the first place. Give me the strength to stop long enough to examine my feelings. I know this may not happen overnight. Sometimes I feel powerless. Since you are a power much greater than myself, I ask for your spirit to fill me always and especially during the times when the hunger wants to rule me.

Will you be with me when I cry? I know you will. I trust you. Let's go. Let's journey. Let's grow. I'm ready and thank you so much that you are with me in every step. Amen.

Why does this partnership have to be so hard?

"WE" is God who is available to all.

As with trying to find one, trying to keep a relationship also has both joy and pain. How can there be more happiness and less friction in your twosome?

Michelle and Derek have been married for almost six years. Derek is a recovering alcoholic with over thirteen years of sobriety. For the most part, they enjoy being together. They do, however, have some problems.

During their first years of marriage, Derek supported Michelle financially and helped her start a business. Derek is self-employed and his 25-year-old company had some financial success in the past. The last several years, however, have been economically devastating. Michelle's income grew and she paid some of Derek's bills rather than take care of her own payables. Michelle struggles to determine where to draw the line between generosity and enabling behavior.

When Derek does not have money for basic living expenses, the pressure builds for both of them. Michelle has become firm in her belief that Derek is able to create income rather than borrow from others. Both of them need help in how to deal with resentment, disappointment and anger.

The good news is that this couple has committed their lives to us and comes to us daily in prayer. As they have increased their level of dedication, they are receiving more of our insight and guidance. Even though they still hang on to certain things that keep them stuck, they also remind each other to honor, cherish and nurture the gift of companionship that they have been given.

After a good night's sleep, when they can get beyond their current worries, they see that their marriage is an opportunity for growth and blessings. Michelle is learning about her codependency and the necessity for detachment with love. Derek thanks us daily for what he has gained through living with Michelle. They have both discovered that, by our grace, they are able to be in a loving, intimate relationship; something neither of them knew was possible before this union.

They handle their troubles through prayer, counseling and surrendering their individual wills to our best for them. We make the difference for Derek and Michelle. We help them find the joy and deal with the pain.

How is your significant relationship? Do you have issues that drag you down? Could you use our guidance? We do not encourage denial. We do not encourage couples to stay together at all costs. There are definite times when marriages should break up. For Michelle and Derek, we keep telling them that we did indeed bring them together. We want them to experience the miracle of our intervention in their lives and marriage.

Try some of the following actions to improve your relationship:
- Develop friendships outside of the marriage, so you do not expect your spouse to be your only friend.
- Talk with one another when you are not plugged-in.
- Even if it feels weird, try praying together.
- Ask us to show you specific actions that you can each take.
- Pray together in the morning and before sleeping.
- Say grace before meals.

Praying together will enhance your awareness that we are with you. You may want to pray the following:

Dear God,

This marriage stuff, whew! Did you really say that it is not good for man or woman to be alone? Sometimes I think that being single would be a heck of a lot easier than trying to work together as a couple. I cannot stand some of the things that my mate does. Other times, I am struck by the sheer joy of living with my best friend. It is invaluable for me to share love, life and touch with this person. Lord, I want us to stay married and grow old together. I don't want to lose all of the caring, history and learning that we have created with each other.

It's just that, God, why does it have to be such a struggle sometimes? On a shallow level, I'd like to say that it is all my partner's fault, that I am right and my partner is wrong. If my way could always happen, then I think our relationship would be so much smoother. Oh yeah. My spouse has another opinion. This is the hard part. I am willing to ask that your will be done, not my will, not my partner's, but yours.

Sometimes, when I am upset, I take it out on my partner and can become so nit-picking. Help me learn how to communicate maturely and to tell the truth in a way that is not mean or hurtful.

Lord, you know that we have times of agreement, love and laughter, too. We have felt you use us as a team to be a blessing to others. Thank you. We want more of those precious moments.

When difficulty comes, Lord, come to help us. Just as soon as we turn our hearts to your power, problem-solving ability and love, we start to feel your hope. You remind us that nothing is impossible through you. We claim that promise, Lord. Help our marriage. Help us trust you. Amen.

Detachment with love

"WE" is God who is available to all.

When you are married, you feel somewhat attached to each other. We support you in learning how to detach with love. Everyone benefits from this action.

Cheryl and Ken are self-employed and work out of their home offices. Ken is a recovering alcoholic. Cheryl is a recovering codependent. Things can get pretty crazy when they start trying to control each other.

When Ken isn't doing work that seems productive, Cheryl gets irritated. Without any request from Ken, Cheryl decides to tell him how he should run his business. Ken feels angry at her condescending, know-it-all attitude.

Then there are times when Ken wants to convince Cheryl to go on a trip rather than put that money into a previously agreed-upon savings account for paying taxes and bills. Her tendencies are to agonize and nag or to give in. She must learn to assertively say no. The relationship will be hurt if Cheryl decides to nag (then Ken can get upset with the nagging and avoid the real issue) or to use the earmarked money for a trip. Being on a vacation is probably more fun than paying bills, but, of course we support Cheryl in keeping the responsible agreement.

Do you ever find yourself dwelling on what another person should do? This could be a thought that she shouldn't buy that dress or that he should apply for a job. What starts out as an innocent wish for someone could turn into a controlling need to dominate. Before you know it, you are spending too much energy on someone else, a person you have no control over. What a waste of your time. What a great way to put stress on the relationship. For you to live a happy life, you've got to let go. When you ask us for our help, we will take away your obsession.

Here are a few actions you could take:

- Ask us to help you detach with love.
- Envision our arms enfolding you and lifting from you the burden of trying to take care of or change another person. Burdens, indeed.
- Ask for our help more than one time. Depending upon the depth of the relationship, you may need to pray to us constantly for a while.
- You may want to pray the following:

Dear God,

Sometimes I get preoccupied with what I think another person should do, think or wear. Help! I don't like giving up so much of my time trying to change someone else. Help me treat each person in my life with the same dignity and respect you give to me. You let me make my own decisions. You are able to let me fail and never take your love away from me.

Detachment is actually quite easy to have with my acquaintances. I am able to watch what they do and not have nearly the same plugged-in feeling I have with my loved one. Part of it is that I care so much. But, I know I am caring inappropriately when my love turns into wanting to control. Then I feel mostly frustration and anger, especially when the person does not do what I want.

I've seen you do miracles in my life on this topic. I've come to you with worry and you have taken away the burden. With your strength, I don't have to act like a victim, either.

Sometimes I need to have tough love. Help me speak with clarity so my partner will understand me when I say no. Help me feel confident in my decisions, so that I am not affected by how my partner responds.

Help me know the difference between nagging and encouraging. Help me know the difference between enabling behavior and kindness.

My first choice is that this person and I stay together. I also ask for your divine wisdom so that I will know if the relationship becomes too difficult for me. If this happens, please show me how to do the most loving and healthy thing. Amen.

section six

Other Life Issues

Patience is a virtue

"WE" is God who is within you.

You know the feeling of wanting something, but having to wait? Maybe patience is a virtue because it can bring you closer to us. When you don't know what is going to happen, you can worry yourself into self-doubt and great pain. Or, you can learn to "let go and let God." The question is, how?

Fran wants to get a manuscript published. She feels grateful to have found what seems to be the perfect agent. Her agent found two interested publishers who are good with first-time writers. The agent hopes to hear something in two weeks. Two weeks turn into four weeks. They haven't said no, so that feels good. But the waiting is a test for Fran. Oh, and the weeks have now turned into months.

On good days Fran thinks, "I know that all will work for good so there is nothing to worry about. The timing is perfect." On so-so days she frets, "Even though I know my agent will call me when she has news, I think I'll call her anyway, just for reassurance." On bad days, Fran agonizes, "Who do I think I am? I can't believe that I thought I had anything that anyone would be interested in reading. Why am I wasting my time writing, anyway?"

You may have heard it said that time isn't literal for us. One day may seem like a thousand years. This is true. We do know the future. However, we do not often tell you. Why? We want you to develop your faith in us. Then you can welcome the waiting. All things work for good when you have surrendered your will to our plan for your life. The hard part comes when you let yourself think of all the worst-case scenarios. When Fran thanks us in advance for charting her course, then she feels the worry leave. Then she is able to continue writing. We remind her that all she needs to do is trust and let go of her agenda.

What are you impatient about? Are you waiting to get test results? Are you hoping that your house will sell? Are you waiting for a check in the mail? Have you been ill for several years, and no one seems to be able to tell you what is wrong? We know about your unique situation and your sleepless nights.

What do you do in the meantime? Although it is not easy, you could use this time to perfect your faith in us. Our ways are higher than your ways. Nothing can separate you from our love. We are bigger than any crises. Some conditions are extremely difficult to handle. If you trust us and believe that we have not left you, this will give you peace.

The next time you find yourself in need of patience, try any of the following:

- Remember that nothing will ever separate you from our love.
- Know that we came for you to have an abundant life, no matter what the current circumstances look like.
- You may take out your anger and frustration with us. We can handle it.
- Ask us to show you how to best deal with the waiting.
- You may want to pray the following:

Dear Lord,

One good thing about the uncertainty in my life is that I spend more time with you in prayer. I am frustrated that sometimes the answer I need is dependent upon other people. Sometimes I start to lose my confidence. Why would anyone want me? Want to hire me? Want to publish my book? Want to pay me? Is anyone able to help me?

I'm going nuts with all of the unknowns. I don't want to act like I'm fine, because I'm not! I'm worried. I wonder, why me? Other people get faster answers and I always have to wait. Well not always, but it seems like it.

If I am having to wait because there is some lesson I need to learn, Lord, show me, show me, show me! To the best of my knowledge, I am willing to do whatever it takes to learn and then to move on!

I've heard that sometimes we are called to have faith even when we don't see the end result. Well, you have never failed me. Actually, it seems as if you are a conductor, directing all of the individual parts of my life. Help me get to the point where I am always trusting you. My life would be much smoother. I do believe in your provision. Help my unbelief! Amen.

How can I balance it all?

"WE" is God who is within you.

One way for you to go crazy is to try to be perfect in everything you do. Although not easy, setting boundaries, taking care of yourself, having realistic expectations and being balanced in the roles you play will help you experience more joy.

Her children's health and well-being are Rose's number one priorities. However, it is still difficult that she can't squeeze in a trip to the gym. She felt sad when she missed the deadline to send in a bid for an exciting graphic arts project. Is it wrong for Rose to want to exercise, to want to use her gifts in a productive way? Need she always put her family before her own desires?

We want to help Rose and you. When you are listening to us, we tell you when you are out of balance. We give you messages such as, "Stop working so hard." "Stop volunteering right now." "Take some time for yourself." "Play with your family." "Get a babysitter and spend time with a friend."

We help you say things like, "Thanks for asking, and I've got to think about it. I'll get back to you." We are that practical in helping you live a balanced life.

We help you learn to say "no." You could be feeling guilty out of an unhealthy notion that you should please everyone and deny yourself. We do not ask you to give more than you are able to contribute. We want you to wake up and be glad for the day, rather than dread your too-long list of things to do.

One of the many areas where you often get out of balance is exercise. When you breathe deeply, it is easier for you to connect with us. We are in the trees, breeze, water and leaves. When you reach, stretch, lift, ride, paddle, swim, hike, run or dance, it is easier for you to speak with us. Ask us to help you determine what, where, when and how to include physical movement into your life.

We are the key to balance. Specific actions you may want to take include:

- Start each day with prayer and meditation, asking for our guidance.
- Before bedtime, recall your accomplishments, rather than magnify the tasks you did not complete.
- Identify your top values. For example, if your number one value is to provide a loving, caring space for the children, when you accomplish this, take the time to feel good about meeting your highest goal.
- Ask family members to give you specific support so that you can live up to these values.
- Schedule movement into your day as one of your most important appointments.
- You may want to pray the following:

Dear God,

Whew! It sounds as if the solution to everything is to be in a relationship with you. Well, that takes time, too! When do I have time to meditate? Your suggestion seems to be just a little bit unrealistic for those of us who have incredibly full lives. I was hoping you'd have better advice for me than, "Spend more time with God."

I want to be more than a half-way decent parent and spouse. I'd like to use my gifts and talents so that I can feel good about myself, too. Sometimes I feel a bit cheated. My children are young so, I have to let them have me when they need me. I come last. Well, that is how it feels sometimes.

There is a subtle message that since my spouse brings in more income than I do, his career is more important than mine. Of course, no one ever says this. But, on down days, I feel it. On top of that, sometimes I feel guilty for complaining because I know that I have much to be thankful for.

Back to me and living a balanced life. Is it possible to lay my head on the pillow at night and feel good about my day? I am so tempted to notice what did not happen. Why can't I feel better about my role as a parent? Many people say that raising a child is next to holiness. I'm sorry, but, I don't always feel holy. Sometimes I feel neglected and used!

Chauffeuring, cooking and cleaning will be in my parent job description for quite a few more years. Help me have peace about these duties, rather than complain about how my talents are being underutilized. I chose to be a parent and it is my dream come true to be able to raise these children. Not a day goes by when I don't thank you for them. OK, so, not a day goes by when I don't utter at least a silent sigh of exasperation at how much time it takes to be a parent. I suppose you hear that, too.

So, what is the answer, Lord? I am committed to this family. I am here for the long haul. I do not want to divorce, or give up my children. I just want a break once in a while. I'd like to excel in something rather than do it only half-way because of my parenting responsibilities.

Seems like either my expectations need to change or I need to carve out a bit more time for me. Lord, help me pinpoint what would help me feel more satisfied. Next, help me explain this to my spouse and children. This could work, because they can be (on good days) quite understanding. It may be an opportunity to show the family that the world does not revolve around them. "Mommy is a person, too." I am actually teaching them an important lesson.

Help me remember that taking care of myself is vital. It is one of the best ways for me to be a good parent, spouse and friend. In fact, you are saying that it is an excellent role model that I can give to my family, to help them learn how to honor and respect another person.

I know that sometimes my desires are conflicting. I need this kind of quiet time to focus on my priorities. Once I get them straight, help me let go of the rest. Lord, for me to feel satisfied and be balanced might not be a fast and easy task. But, I've got to make some progress. Help me. I trust that you will. Amen.

Having ADD and learning to pay attention to God

"WE" is God who is within you.

Have you ever tried to accomplish something but the outcome does not seem worth the amount of effort you put into it? What about the feeling that your life is becoming nothing more than "spinning your wheels"? Imagine what it would be like to have these feelings most of the time. It would be lonely, depressing and tiring.

We help you to see that not fitting into society's norms can actually be a blessing. We help you discover the special calling that you had only thought about, but were too scared to pursue. We do not promise that there will be no pain in life. Rather, in the midst of your struggle, we can bring healing and even joy. Let us tell you about Chris.

Chris grew up with a learning disorder and did not discover what it was until he was twenty-six years old. He always felt inadequate when he compared himself with his peers. Afraid to be called "dumb," he sometimes cheated to get good grades in junior and senior high school.

His low self-esteem in the classroom carried over into his social life. Chris hated himself and viewed his future with despair. In fact, Chris often thought about ending his life. At times it was only his faith in us that kept him going. At other times, even this faith was shaky: "God, are you there? Do you care about me?"

Almost every night he talked with us, asking questions and telling us about his problems. Because Chris constantly tried to improve and break out of his perpetual rut, he paid close attention to the things around him. He started to notice an answer in a sign.

He interpreted it as, "Just keep going." He was unsure if it was really a sign or if he was making it up in his head. But later, other things appeared in signs only he could decipher. He continued his dreary life and often asked why he should. The answers came back, "Do not quit, just keep going."

At times, Chris was certain that he heard our voice. Other times, he was not sure. We want to assure you that this is normal. There is enough competition for your listening, that sometimes our quiet voice does not get heard.

Although most classes were extremely difficult for him, Chris suffered through college. He wanted to please his parents and prove to himself that he could do it. He anguished with many thoughts of checking out but knew that we wanted him to live, that we had much for him to learn. He got through schools without being tested for a disorder partly due to his people-pleasing ability, his learned athletic skills and his sheer will.

After graduation he found a job that many people would have loved, but he was miserable most of the time. Then one day, we presented the idea to him that his mind really was different. He was subsequently diagnosed with attention deficit disorder (ADD).

Relieved to gain this explanation, Chris started to feel thankful, even though it was a long, hard journey. He adapted the view, "If I would have discovered my ADD earlier, I would not have experienced the years of pain which now give me an understanding for those who have similar problems." When he provides a parent or child support in how to better deal with a learning disorder, Chris is very pleased.

His persistence in listening to us enables him to see purpose and feel joy. He no longer dwells on the things he can't do well. Instead, he is discovering, developing and using the talents he has.

Chris learned that those with ADD are more skilled in some areas than other people are. He enjoys the opportunity to do complex problem solving. Part of his career will probably always involve working with children which is fun for him because of the variety and action needed. He has developed confidence in his ability to persevere, and eventually succeed, even if it is through the side door.

Achieving a new attitude includes brutal, dogged determination. Chris couldn't bear the thought of continuing to live with so much self-doubt, guilt, worry and despair. He decided to trust that we did not make a mistake in creating him, even with ADD.

He now wakes up feeling glad to be alive, rather than not wanting to get out of bed, which is how he felt for over twenty years of his life. He is noticing a shift from always questioning to accepting that we are in his life. Does he ever have a bad day? Of course. Does he ever regret the choices he makes? Surely. Having ADD still presents some challenges, too. However, Chris looks at a difficult situation these days and knows that we will help him deal with it. Nothing is as bad when you know that you are not alone.

Just as Chris has learned to accept the uniqueness of who he is, you can do the same. We want you to grow daily in loving who you are. It is a lifetime journey. Gratitude is not a state of mind that will come to you overnight. There will be days when you feel low. Chris makes it through each day by being in a relationship with us and trusting that we have a plan for his good. It takes faith.

Listed below are several actions you could take that may help you or someone you care about deal with ADD or any special learning challenge:

- Review the pain of your past. Find someone you can talk to or write about it. Let us be your source of healing so that you can let go of your anger, sadness, regret and resentment.

- Discover what is special about you. How are you with problem solving? Do you have a keen sense of smell? Can you wholeheartedly play and enjoy being with children? Do you have a special love for animals?
- Find someone who has ADD and help that person with the struggle. Share your empathy with those who cheat because they feel trapped and torn, for those who hate life because they feel helpless.
- You may want to pray the following:

Dear God,

Thank you for my ADD. I don't always feel grateful. But I want to try. You have blessed me with unique talents. While I could tell the world about the areas where I feel deficient, now is the time for me to notice my gifts. Help me see my positive qualities. Actually, there are a few things I can do that seem easier for me than for most people! I've just never put much attention on them.

I've almost gotten used to dwelling on my weaknesses. I am now ready to switch my focus! Self-hatred sucks! It also sucks when I am always trying to hide who I really am. I would love to be in love with life and in love with whom you have created: Me. Can you help me with self-love? I will guess that your answer is yes. Help me wake up with a new, thankful attitude.

Lord, this is a journey that I don't think will happen overnight. I still want to take it. Be with me. Be in me. Lead and guide me. I will look for your signs. I want to feel your love. I want to experience your healing of my years of sadness. I am coming to you daily for guidance and assurance. Let's go! Amen.

Cancer, an equal opportunity disease

"WE" is God who is within you.

For many of you, cancer is a disease that attacks "other" people. Some of you, however, are intimately aware of how cancer can strike close to home.

Ron was tired for most of the spring. It took three appointments before his doctor could determine the cause. Cancer was detected. Only 41 years old, Ron and his family were shocked.

Of course there is never a good time for disease. Ron had feelings of disbelief and anger but didn't hang on to them very long. He is more aware than ever before of what it means to have the love and support of family and friends. The kind touch of a back rub when he is stiff from lying on the couch feels so good.

He knows that his family would do anything for him. For this, he is grateful. He hopes that he won't ever take for granted the things that really matter.

Before the cancer, Ron was quite the joker. He wishes that he could laugh more now, but much of his energy is expended in trying to get well.

Strangers gawk at his bald head and slim physique and Ron comments, "I'm much more aware of how rude it is to stare!" The sight of his gaunt figure in the mirror reminds him that he must eat. Unfortunately, not much tastes good anymore. Ron prays that he can keep up his hope, especially on the low days.

Our words to follow are for Ron and for all others who are suffering with cancer or other illnesses:

Dear Ron,

We love you. We understand how you feel. When you ask us for help, we give you emotional comfort and at times we give you physical relief. We do not promise spontaneous healing for everyone. It will always be a mystery why some are healed and why some are not. Your body is sick, but your spirit is whole and will live forever. Some people with cancer have grown closer to us. Others have decided that we do not exist.

This choice of how to believe is, of course, up to you. Knowing us is an act of faith. You may not feel anything. We come to you now and anytime you call. Some say that our presence is what gives them peace in the midst of pain and illness. We want you to experience this peace that passes all understanding.

Faith is believing without seeing. Believe that we will never leave you and that we will help you deal with everything. This is our prayer for you.

The following is a prayer that Ron and others who are hurting can pray:

Dear God,

Having faith in you sounds too good to be true. Is there really a source that can give me peace in the midst of all of this uncertainty? How do you do that? Oh yeah, by faith.

If you are an intuition inside me, it sounds like I can "make you up." I can pretend there is a God and then talk with him. Why would I use my energy to do this? I'm sorry to sound like a pain, but, I need to know. Do you care that I have cancer? Can you help me? What do you require of me in return? If I get healed, will I have to go to church and wear a "Jesus Saves" tee shirt?

Is it not like that? You mean that there is not a list of requirements for me if I start believing in you? Is there not a certain church that I must join?

I just want the feeling of not being alone. Also, I need all the help I can get, especially if my cancer progresses. Will you help me have as little pain as possible?

I'd like to believe that if I die, I will go to another place better than this one. Or else, I could believe that when I die, I'm gone and that is it. Of those two choices, the living forever one sounds better. I like the idea of a heavenly place without pain or illness.

Of course, having all the cancer leave my body is my first choice. I've heard of cases where it goes away. If there are certain foods that will help me live, I'll eat them! Lord, help me do all I can to be healed. I'd love to live fully for many, many more years. If attitude has anything to do with my recovery, give me a strong faith in your provision. The thought that this cancer could be licked is thrilling to me. I do not know what is going to happen. So, team up with me, Lord. Don't leave me now.

You are ultimately in control. I do not know the future, but I would like to trust that you know the best future for me. Your will be done. Amen.

Conclusion: What next?

"WE" is God who is within you.

If you have a sense that being in a relationship with us feels right, this could be because we created you. We are the creator and you are our creation. We would love to be in communion with you. However, this must be your choice. Whatever your decision is, we love you just as much. We are not concerned about your membership in heaven. Heaven is now. You are already in.

Do we really have interest in your day-to-day affairs? Aren't we busy with more important work? Our word to you is simple. We care.

Some of you would prefer to call the inner intelligence your own intuition rather than the voice of God. That is fine. We do not care what you call us.

Many mysteries are not uncovered in this book. Some persons are healed. Others die. Bad jobs happen. Relationships fall apart. We come to help you in the stuff of life. We do not promise happiness, but we do offer peace and inner joy. As we said in chapter one, may you hear our answers to your questions as you open your mind and meditate on our presence in your life.

You may recognize that some phrases in this book are from the Bible. We wrote the Bible through people years ago. Please don't ever make those words more important than our spirit of love that inspired the words.

Certain chapters that may offend some of you are not meant to be offensive. More than a few souls have suffered because of judgments made in our name. We can only be love.

We are not judgment.

We are always looking for those who want to be used. That is how we found the recorder for this book which, by the way, went through several revisions. Why wasn't it perfect in draft one since this information is from us? It took our human scribe a while to write what we wanted to convey. We have no problem with editing when it makes the message clearer.

The anecdotes you read are a combination of real people's experiences. Perhaps you found a few stories that were similar to happenings in your own life. When your situation is different, ask us to speak directly to you about your unique circumstance.

Some of you are tired of introspection. You have a heart for those less fortunate and are ready to help the poor, hungry and homeless. This desire is our spirit stirring in you.

What do we recommend? Share our love. Share our message of hope and healing. This can be done in many ways. Tell us that you want our guidance and we'll tell you what comes next. When you dedicate yourself to us, we gladly return to you fun, learning, newness, awe, joy, creativity, meaning and the feeling of being alive.

As you read this page, we are fluttering around you. Invite us to share your life with you for the first time or the one-hundredth. We're ready. Let's go!

Epilogue

Writing this book has been a journey of faith. It takes faith to follow the voice of God. The answers—even as they feel true and right—may not always be logical. My friend Deb says, "they may even be difficult."

Recently I received a message to do something that indeed felt right but at the same time very difficult. I have free will when it comes to following this guidance. My decision to move ahead comes from a belief that it is for the best.

I feel amazingly cared for while doing this hard thing. I am experiencing the peace that passes all understanding which is available not just to me but to all of us, when we ask for divine help.

Contained in this book are some examples of life's challenges. All I can say is that with God, it won't be as hard as without God. With God, there will be an inner peace even while you are crying. May you experience the rich, deep knowing that nothing can ever happen that will separate you from God's love. That is what transports us to joy.

The very best to you as you travel on the path of listening and following. As we increase our level of dedication to God, there will be less pain and more joy. Blessings to you on your journey.

Aloha,
Nancy Hanson

About the writer

Nancy Hanson grew up in a Midwestern, mostly Lutheran, largely Scandinavian community, not unlike Lake Wobegon. She was taught that there is a loving God who longs to be in a personal relationship with everyone. Believing in God came naturally to Nancy, who saw faith as a great way to reduce anxiety. Her favorite verse was and still is, "Don't worry about anything; instead, pray about everything. If you do this you will experience God's peace, which is far more

wonderful than the human mind can understand."

Nancy received a bachelor's degree in psychology and social work from Concordia College, Moorhead, Minnesota, and a master's degree in counseling and guidance from Pacific Lutheran University, Tacoma, Washington. While in graduate school, she worked as a church youth director and was subsequently employed in youth ministry.

As much as Nancy loved church work, she followed an inner guidance to switch her focus to career development. She started her own company, Career Discovery, and has worked for ten years as a career counselor, writer and speaker. Nan counsels clients in career transition, including people getting out of the military services. As a former Drake Beam Morin, Inc. outplacement consultant, Nan presented workshops for those downsized from companies including American Express, Chevron, IBM, U.S. Sprint,

Verifone and Xerox. She has taught career development courses for counselors at Chaminade University and the University of Hawaii. Ms. Hanson is a nationally certified career counselor and member of the National Speakers Association. She is also a contributing writer for the *Honolulu Advertiser's* "At Work In Hawaii" column.

Her first book, *Create Work You Love*, came out in 1995. Wanting to reach more people with a spiritual message, Nan wrote *From Pain to Joy*.

Nancy is available to speak to groups about her books and is known for integrating humor and music into presentations that offer great insight.

Suggested reading and listening

Alcoholics Anonymous World Services. *Alcoholics Anonymous "The Big Book."* 3rd ed. New York: Alcoholics Anonymous World Services, 1976.

Colgrove, Melba; Bloomfield, Harold; McWilliams, Peter. *How to Survive the Loss of a Love.* Los Angeles, CA: Prelude Press, 1991.

Courage to Change. New York: Al-Anon Family Group Headquarters, Inc., 1992.

The Dalai Lama. *The Way to Freedom.* New York: HarperCollins Publishers, 1994.

Daniel, Alma; Ramer, Andrew; Wyllie, Timothy. *Ask Your Angels.* New York: Ballantine Books, 1992.

Dyer, Wayne - anything by him, especially - *Manifesting Your Destiny.* New York: HarperCollins, 1997. Or, order the cassette tape version from Nightingale-Conant at 1-800-525-9000.

Food for Thought. Hazelden Foundation, 1980.

Fox, Matthew - anything by him, especially - *Confessions.* New York: HarperCollins, 1996.

Goldsmith, Joel S. *The Art Of Meditation.* New York: HarperCollins, 1956.

Grant, Amy - everything by her, including - *Behind The Eyes.* Hollywood, CA: A&M Records, Inc., 1997.

Greene, Bob and Winfrey, Oprah. *Make The Connection.* New York: Hyperion, 1996.

Griffin, John Howard. *Follow the Ecstasy, The Hermitage Years of Thomas Merton.* Maryknoll, New York: Orbis Books, 1993.

Hanh, Thich Nhat. *Peace Is Every Step*. New York: Bantam, 1991.

Hendrix, Harville. *Getting The Love You Want*. New York: Henry Holt & Company, 1988.

Maddox, Rebecca. *Inc. Your Dreams*. New York: Penguin Books, 1995.

Mazzoleni, Don Mario. *A Catholic Priest Meets Sai Baba*. Faber, VA: Leela Press Inc., 1991.

Millman, Dan - anything by him, especially - *Everyday Enlightenment*. New York: Warner Books, 1998 and *The Laws of Spirit*. Tiburon, CA: HJ Kramer, 1995.

Moore, Thomas. *SoulMates*. New York: HarperCollins, 1994.

Mundis, Jerrold. *How to Get Out of Debt, Stay Out of Debt and Live Prosperously*. New York: Bantam, 1988.

Percy, Ian - anything by him, especially - *Going Deep: Exploring Spiritually in Life and Leadership*. Toronto, Ontario, Canada: Macmillan Canada, 1997.

Russell, A.J., editor. *God Calling*. New York: The Berkley Publishing Group, 1972.

Sher, Barbara - anything by her, especially - *It's Only Too Late If You Don't Start Now*. New York: Delacorte Press, 1998.

Siegel, Bernie. *Love, Medicine and Miracles*. New York: Harper & Row, 1986.

The Living Bible. Wheaton, IL: Tyndale House Publications, 1971.

Tieger, Paul D. and Barbara Barron-Tieger. *Do What You Are*. New York: Little, Brown & Company, 1992.

Wilber, Ken. *Grace and Grit*. Boston, MA: Shambhala Publications, Inc., 1991.

How to purchase *From Pain to Joy*

Within the State of Hawaii:

Send your name and address, $10, plus shipping* to:
    From Pain to Joy
    4224 Waialae Avenue #5-275
    Honolulu, Hawaii 96816
    (808) 942-1628 / (888) 807-9494 toll free
*Shipping: $2.00 for the first book and $1.00 for each additional book.
Make checks payable to *From Pain to Joy*

Or, visit a local bookstore such as:

Unity Bookstore	New Day Books
3608 Diamond Head Circle	109 Kekili
Honolulu, Hawaii 96815	Kailua, Hawaii 96734
(808) 735-6116	(808) 262-7456
M-F 10-4 Saturdays closed	M-Sat 10-5
Sundays 8:30 AM to 1:00 PM	Sundays closed

Or, purchase books from The Movement Center, whose goal is to integrate body, mind and spirit through the performing arts. All of your $10 will go to this worthy cause. Order by contacting: Ms. Lisa Tuttle, 1629 Wilder Avenue #604, Honolulu Hawaii, 96822-4666, (808) 946-0357.

Outside of Hawaii: You may purchase this book on the internet at http://www.amazon.com or call toll free (888) 265-2732.

From Pain to Joy will soon be out in an audio version. Let us know if you would like to order this.

Tell your friends that they can read selected chapters of this book on the internet at www.career-discovery.com